Sinister Swamps

Monsters and Mysteries from the Mire

Lyle Blackburn

An Original Publication of LegendScape Publishing

Sinister Swamps: Monsters and Mysteries from the Mire

ISBN: 978-1-7349206-0-4

Cover art by Claudio Bergamin (www.bergaminart.com)

- Dedicated to Thomas Wayne Shirley

Illustrations by artists as credited

Photos courtesy of individual photographers as credited

Edited by Beth Wojiski (www.wojiski.com)

Proofreading by Craig Woolheater

Print design by Lyle Blackburn

For more information about the author, visit:

www.lyleblackburn.com

Follow the author at:

www.facebook.com/lyleblackburn.official

www.twitter.com/BlackburnLyle

www.instagram.com/lyleblackburn

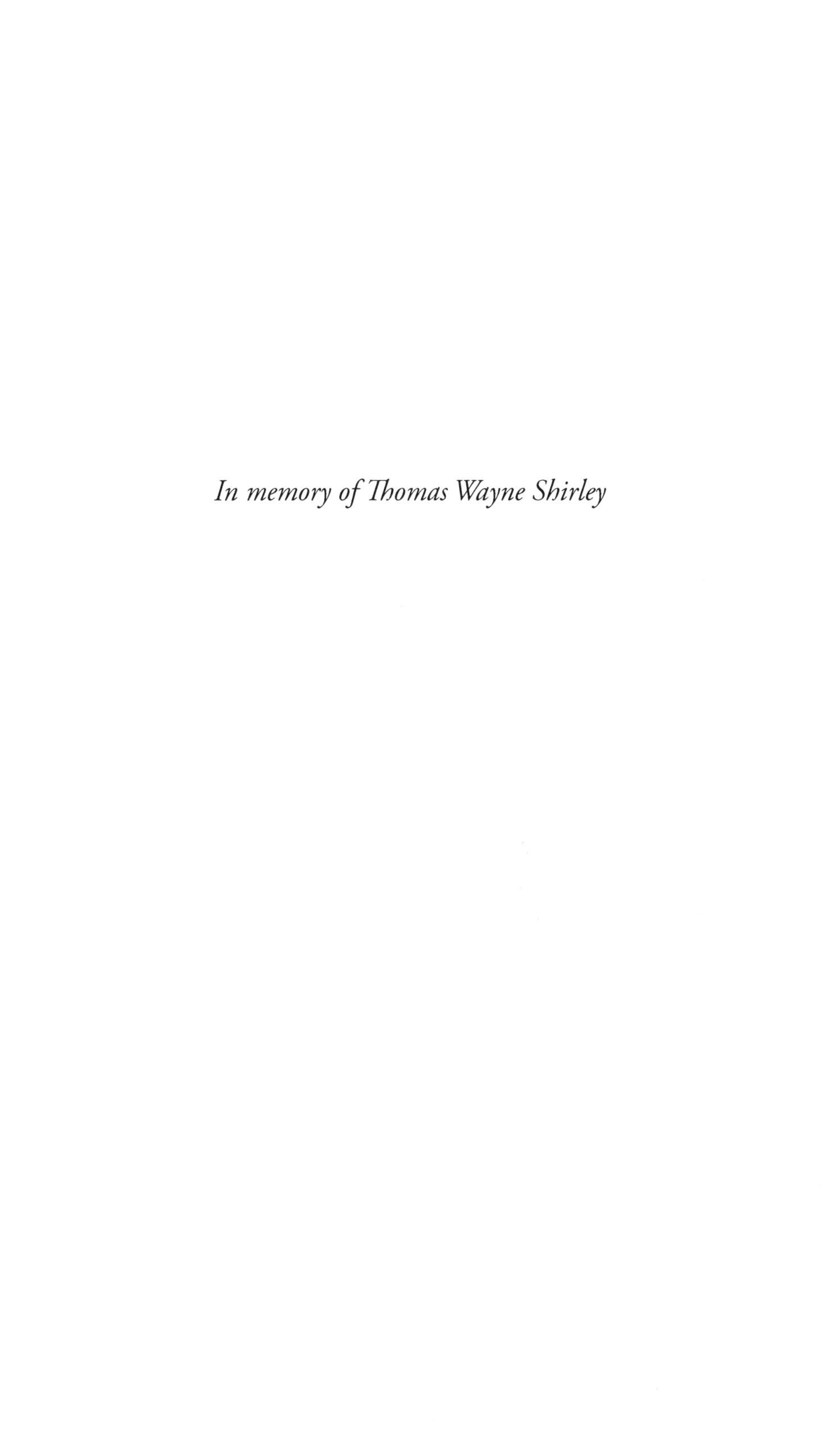

In memory of Thomas Wayne Shirley

CONTENTS

INTRODUCTION

I was ten years old when my parents and grandparents decided to rent an RV and embark on the ultimate family vacation to Florida. We lived in Texas (as I still do), so this was to be an unprecedented road-trip adventure culminating in stops at White Sands Beach, Silver Springs, Key West, the Everglades, and of course, Walt Disney World. I still have fond memories of the trip, which looking back was quite an undertaking with five adults, myself, and my sister crammed into a modest-sized RV for hours upon end as we traversed the far reaches of Florida making our way to the various destinations.

Disney World was the main attraction for us kids at the time, yet I found myself enjoying the slew of side stops with as much thrill as the mouse ears and amusement rides. It was during these interim adventures that I was first introduced to a real-life swamp. The first taste came at Silver Springs Park located west of the Ocala National Forest. Silver Springs was the oldest tourist attraction in Florida, which had also been used as the set for Hollywood's *Tarzan* movies of the 1930s and 1950s. Among its various attractions, Silver Springs offered glass-bottom boat tours, a reptile house, alligators, and a boardwalk known as Cypress Point. I can still recall my first glimpse of the boardwalk's stately cypress trees towering above the water amid a backdrop of moss-covered limbs and moonlight. It was a place of wonder like none I'd ever seen. For a few bucks I was able to hold a small boa constrictor while they snapped a souvenir photo and placed it in a commemorative paper frame decorated with a drawing of an alligator. The photo remains a treasure of my early childhood adventures.

While Cypress Point offered a beginner's view of Florida swampland, it wasn't the ultimate plunge into a marshy wilderness. That would come just a few days later when we rolled into Florida's famed Everglades National Park. Upon our arrival, my grandfather—who always seemed to know exactly what I would enjoy most on vacations—chartered an airboat to take us deep into the 'Glades. I can still recall my delight as we sailed over miles of reed grass and floated slowly under cypress canopies as the boat howled and growled its way through the watery terrain. As a boy accustomed to the dry expanses of central Texas, this was a world away; something I had only seen on television prior to visiting Florida. It was during this particular outing that my imagination formed a lifetime bond with the murky bogs of American swampland that has continued to this day.

Swamps such as the Everglades have long been a subject of wonder and fascination. There's something about this unique ecosystem that oozes with intrigue as it offers a glimpse into a primordial past. Within the landscapes of moss-draped trees and brackish waters, nature displays some of its finest work from an array of amazing, aquatic vegetation to a multitude of winged, webbed, finned, furred, and often dangerous inhabitants. It's a place that can just as easily spark one's scientific curiosity as it does one's fears. It's a place like no other where scenic beauty and imminent peril seem to coexist in perfect harmony.

By night, the swamp takes on an even creepier appearance as the fingered branches of cypress trees, ghostly moss, and blackened waters blend with a din of strange noises and guttural calls from its shadowy denizens. For this reason swamps have often been used as the backdrop for television shows or horror movies where an extra air of spookiness is required. Traditional tales of folklore and fiction have also utilized the setting to great effect. Placing a ghost story or monster tale firmly within a swamp went a long way toward striking fear into the heart of listeners or readers. Famous horror authors such as H.P. Lovecraft knew the power of swampscapes, mentioning places such as the Big Cypress Swamp in his stories. In fact, Lovecraft once joined a fellow writer in search of a mysterious place called "Dark Swamp," which was rumored to exist between Rhode Island and Connecticut. The legend surrounding the place is said to have influenced the opening of Lovecraft's story "The Colour Out of Space."

The ominous reputation of the swamp is not confined to the realms of fiction, however. Swamps are also places where real-life mysteries and spooky legends flourish. Rumors of monsters, ghosts, witches, and even buried treasure are often rooted in their bubbling backwaters. Though some are inevitably entangled with local lore, many transcend rumors through eyewitness reports, tangible evidence, and occasionally a photo.

Over the years, more than a few swampland visitors claim to have encountered strange beasts or animals unknown to the outside world. These creatures, which typically fall into the category of cryptozoology (the study of unproven animals), run the gamut from ape-like humanoids to shadowy felines to devilish dogs to slithering aquatic forms and winged wonders that defy rational explanation. Others have reported experiences with ghosts, spook lights, and other haunted phenomena. Perhaps this is not surprising given that swamps are often associated with cases of missing persons, tragic deaths, and hidden bodies. And buried treasure? This, too, seems curiously plausible since swamps are the ideal place to hide that which needs to be hidden.

Since my eye-opening trip to Silver Springs and the Everglades, I have visited a considerable number of swampy habitats over the years, including some much closer to my old home than

I could have ever imagined. During these adventures, which have ranged from simply canoeing the waters to extensive hikes and camping excursions, I've not only enjoyed the ambiance of these boggy landscapes but sought to learn more about the mysteries they may hold—a passion that has resulted in this book.

Swamps, it seems, are a world away within our reach, offering hope that there are things out there we have yet to understand. Join me now for an eerie exploration into this unique landscape as I part the mossy curtains and expose the sinister secrets within some of North America's most notorious swamplands.

1

HOCKOMOCK

The moon glared overhead as Officer Hadley drove along the deserted, two-lane road. A ghostly fog was settling in, so he proceeded with caution, though he rarely passed other motorists on his nightly commute. Hadley worked the evening shift as a correctional officer for a Massachusetts prison facility and had traversed the route many times over the years. It was something he enjoyed. After nine hours within the confines of cinder block walls and captive tension, a peaceful drive through wooded backroads had a calming effect. On this particular night, however, his peaceful respite would be shattered by an unexpected encounter.

It was October 2016. The gauzy air that evening was not enough to obscure visibility, but it was enough to cast a rather unusual pall over the winding road, which ran west of Foxborough. The area here is engulfed by thick trees and flanked by a vast, swampy bottomland. As Hadley traveled, his headlights would occasionally reflect off the standing water like glints of scattered treasure.

Hadley had just rounded a bend and was looking ahead when something darted from the swamp on the right and bounded across the road in full view of his headlights. It was a huge, dog-like creature running in a hunched-over fashion with its head low. Hadley instinctively tapped his brakes as the thing ran into the trees on the opposite side of the road, disappearing into the blackness.

The encounter was brief, but enough for the officer to get a good look at the beast. Though it was dog-like, he was sure it was not a dog. Nor was it a coyote or even a wolf. This thing was much larger and unusual with dark fur and a body like a hyena.

On all fours it was as tall as the hood of his Nissan Altima, and if it had been standing, it was probably seven feet in height. It moved both like a canid and an ape and was altogether unlike anything he'd ever seen.

"From my peripheral vision, I caught it just as it came in front of my car," Hadley told me in a series of conversations. "It was hunched over and moving fast."

Hadley estimated the thing passed a mere ten feet in front of his vehicle, giving him a close-up view. "It had high shoulders, low back hips and haunches like a dog's back legs," he said. "The back legs were working together like a dog, but its front legs were running independent of each other, like when you see a gorilla charge."

Hadley didn't see much of the face, but he could see the head was pointed downward, as if it were hunting. The body was covered in "long, gray fur like a dog" with "dark, black skin on its underbelly." He could see a tail behind it, but couldn't tell if it was tucked between its legs or if it was just a short, one-foot-long appendage. The creature was so big he mainly focused on its center mass. Whatever it was, it was completely unnerving.

"When it passed me, the hair on my arms went up and something in my body was telling me to go," he confessed. "I work in the prisons and I don't get scared easily. But when I saw this thing, my body went into a fight-or-flight response."

Anyone in Hadley's position would probably have had the same reaction. The beast was monstrous and frightening, even from within the relative safety of the car. Luckily it seemed to pay him no mind as it dashed into the foggy woods. After a few stunned moments, the officer accelerated and left the area as quickly as he could.

While it's impossible to know just what kind of creature Hadley encountered that night, it does not seem typical of the fauna found upon the North American landscape. Its size and combination of hyena, wolf, and ape-like characteristics don't necessarily rule out a practical explanation, but when viewed in context of both the bizarre anatomy and the location of the encounter, it does lend itself to possibilities beyond the norm. Perhaps its origin can be traced to an infamous bog that lies just a few scant miles away.

Enter the Triangle

The location where Hadley encountered the strange creature is on the outskirts of one of America's most infamous bottomlands known as the Hockomock Swamp. The Hockomock and its associated habitat encompass nearly 17,000 acres, making it the largest vegetated freshwater wetland system in Massachusetts.[1] Aside from the swamp itself, the system is comprised of rivers, creeks, lakes, ponds, and wetlands whose tendrils reach out to the very road where Hadley drives on his nightly commute.

As a swampland habitat, Hockomock is not unlike others where tangled roots, dense trees, and flooded marshes abound. But in terms of monstrous mysteries and strange happenings, its reputation is nearly unparalleled. From within its spooky boundaries, stories of strange creatures and ghostly happenings have oozed forth for generations to establish a continuous trend of paranormal presence.

Dog-like creatures, such as the one Hadley encountered, are part of its reputed menagerie, along with an assortment of other strange beasts including man-like apes, prehistoric-looking birds, phantom wildcats, giant snakes, and a goblinesque creature known as the Pukwudgie. These creatures, often referred to as "cryptids," are yet to be proven, but are no less real in the eyes of those who have witnessed them in and around the swamp.

Hockomock is also known for sightings of strange lights and ghostly entities which are said to roam its black rivers and muddy marshes. These include glowing orbs hovering along an old railroad track and apparitions of Native Americans that have been seen paddling canoes upon its dark waters. UFOs have also been reported in its vicinity.

Hockomock is at the epicenter of an even broader area of interest known as the "Bridgewater Triangle." The Triangle has been identified as a geographical region spanning approximately two hundred square miles where countless unusual phenomena and sinister activity have taken place. Along with sightings of monstrous beasts, ghostly apparitions, and UFOs, the triangle has been the site of grisly murders and cult rituals, making it one of the most ominous locales in America.

Native Americans were the first people to populate the area and recognize the swamp's life-giving value and otherworldly nature. The very name bestowed upon it by the indigenous Wampanoag tribe, "Hockomock," translates to "place where spirits dwell" in their Algonquian language. According to wildlife journalist Ted Williams, these early inhabitants worshipped the swamp as much they depended on it for sustenance. In their minds, Hockomock hosted "not only the evil spirits that struck terror into paleface hearts, but the good spirits that led [them] to moose and deer."[2]

When European settlers began moving into the area, they had a more singular view of the Hockomock, calling it "Devil's Swamp." Their trepidation was based not only on the foreboding maze of vines, trees, and quicksand, but on its very inhabitants. During the seventeenth century, the Wampanoags used the swamp as a strategic base for their raiding parties as they waged a bloody battle with the English for control of the land.[3] The black spruce trees concealed the painted warriors, who blended with the environment like human chameleons.

Early settlers begin to notice other strange things in the vicinity of the swamp. The first was an "eerie sulfurous yellow light" that filled the sky above Hockomock on several occasions.[4] They referred to the occurrence as "Yellow Day." In 1760, Bridgewater residents saw a "sphere of fire" moving across the sky one morning at 10:00 a.m. It was bright enough to cast a shadow in the sunlight. It also generated a strange sound.[5]

The weird incidents continued into modern times as they began to immortalize the reputation of this sinister swamp. In 1908, on Halloween night no less, two undertakers were traveling by carriage in the vicinity of Hockomock when they noticed a strange object like a "giant lantern" hovering in the sky.[6] They watched it for approximately forty minutes as it moved up and down and in circles.

In 1939, area workers were subject to a much closer encounter, this time with a slithering beast. While working on a construction project near the swamp, several Civilian Conservation Corps personnel claimed to see a huge, black snake "as thick as a stove-pipe."[7] According to the report, the snake coiled up and raised its head for a moment before retreating into the swamp's shadows. The sighting, along with others, reinforced a local legend that a monstrous serpent would appear every seven years in the swamp.

Such intervals of regularity tend to relegate such sightings to the realm of legend more than fact, but periodic reappearances of Hockomock's dark denizens cannot be denied. The dog-like beast Officer Hadley saw in 2016 seems eerily similar to a beast reported in the area in 1976. That year, Phillip Kane, a firefighter living near Abington, saw an animal he described as a "huge black killer dog" standing over the bodies of his two prized ponies.[8] The beast had ripped out their throats and was gnawing on their flesh. Kane fired his pistol at the animal, but missed. The bloodthirsty beast turned and ran into the forest.

In the days that followed, police received an overwhelming number of calls from local citizens who had also spotted the beast in the area. It was enough to set off an intense search to track down what authorities dismissed as "part German Shepherd and part Doberman Pinscher."

Citizens armed themselves as fears grew. This resulted in a young girl being shot in the leg by her brother while he was unloading a firearm. He said he was using the weapon as protection "in case the dog entered their yard."

Meanwhile, policed searched the woods each day until sundown, but were never able to track down the beast and kill it. The dog was last seen by patrolman Francis Curran as it prowled along a railroad track. Curran said he fired at it with his 12-gauge shotgun from a distance of approximately seventy-five yards. The beast seemed to be unfazed by the blast. It turned and slowly walked into the woods, never to be seen again.

If not for the torn throats of the ponies, one might suggest the beast was nothing more than a menacing phantom. This, too, may not seem out of the ordinary in the wilds of Hockomock. In 1988 a witness reported that he was driving on a road in the area when a "huge dog with piercing red eyes" leapt in front of the car. The driver braced for impact, but the animal went right through the vehicle as if it were nothing more than an apparition.[9]

Hair-Raising Hominoids

While reports of giant snakes, killer dogs, and even phantom cats have left their mark on Hockomock's history, perhaps none have been more prevalent than sightings of a hairy, Sasquatch-like hominoid. One of the oldest of these accounts comes from Carlston Wood, who will never forget what he saw in 1970. Carlston was ten years old at the time and lived with his family in an old colonial home on the eastern edge of the swamp. That winter Carlston and two other kids—a girl his age and a boy a few years younger—ventured into the swamp to play near what is known as West Meadow Pond. They were about a mile into the woods when they were startled by a tall figure standing a short distance away. It appeared to be covered in hair and was upright on two legs like a human.

"Almost simultaneously, we noticed something," Wood told me in a personal interview. "It was very tall and had reddish-brown, matted hair." Terrified, the kids turned and ran as fast as they could back home and told their parents. The parents, as expected, dismissed the incident as childhood imagination. But the kids knew what they had seen.

"We didn't know at that time what it was," Wood explained. "But I know now it looked like something very similar to what is described as a Sasquatch creature."

He told me he considered the possibility of a bear, but it simply did not have the right anatomy. "It was so tall and standing upright with almost the same proportions as a human."

Whatever it was, Carlston and his friends were not the only ones to see it. Over the course of the year other residents in the area caught glimpses of what they believed to be a "huge bear" lurking in and around the swamp.[10] The reports were enough to prompt local and state police agencies to organize a search for the animal. For two days they scoured the woods with the aid of hunting dogs but were unable to find it.

The case was investigated by my colleague and prominent cryptid researcher, Loren Coleman, who spoke to witnesses and police officers at the time. As a result of those interviews, Coleman determined it must have been a "very unusual bear" since it was often seen walking upright.[11] (Not to mention the only bear species to ever inhabit New England is the black bear—*Ursus americanus*—and at the time they had been essentially eradicated from the area by hunters.)

The situation culminated with a bizarre incident involving the police themselves. While two officers were sitting idle in their patrol car, they felt something move the back of the vehicle.

"Something began to pick up the rear of our car," the officer explained to a news reporter at the time.[12] "I spun the car around and got my spotlight on something that looked like a bear running on the corner of a house." The elusive "bear" was never found.

By the late 1970s, Joseph DeAndrade—a man who would become an important figure in Bridgewater Triangle research—began to take interest in the mysteries of Hockomock. He often fished around the swamp and on one occasion met a fellow fisherman who told him an incredible story. The young man, Miran, said he was hunting in the swamp with his uncle when they shot what they thought was a bear. When the bullet struck it, the animal made a "very loud and terrifying sound of pain that sounded half animal and half human" and then ran off into the woods.[13] They rushed to the area where the creature had been standing and found "long brown hair and red blood on some leaves." Puzzled by the strange cry and uncharacteristic hair, they began to wonder if the animal was something other than a bear.

Intrigued by the story, DeAndrade began exploring the swamp in hopes of finding evidence of the odd creature. On most occasions he neither found nor saw anything, but that changed in 1978. That winter he and a friend were focusing on the area of Clay Banks Pond on the east side of Hockomock. As they were standing with their backs to the pond, DeAndrade felt an overwhelming urge to turn around. He wasn't sure how to rationalize the urge, but nonetheless turned around and looked across the water. There, on the opposite bank, he saw what appeared to be a large, hair-covered creature walking in a very strange fashion.

"I was in shock at what I saw!" DeAndrade recalled.[14] "It was very tall with long, dark brown hair." He could see its back from the waist up at a distance of about two hundred feet. DeAndrade immediately got the attention of his friend and told him to look across the pond. When they both looked back, the thing was gone.

"I never saw its face since it was walking very slowly down a hill as it was facing a river on the other side," he explained. "From what I saw, I'd say that it was no less than six [feet] tall. [It] might have been the same creature that Miran's uncle had shot."

After they realized the creature wasn't going to reappear, DeAndrade and his companion hiked to the other side of the pond. There they found an area with a downward grade where the thing must have been walking. This seemed to explain the strange, slow pace. It was obviously navigating down a hill.

DeAndrade pondered "the possibility of a person walking around in a monkey costume," but from what he could see, it did not appear to be any sort of costume or jacket.[15] By all accounts he'd seen Hockomock's hairy man-beast, a creature whose legend was just beginning.

Following the event, DeAndrade became even more focused on his research. Not only did he continue to explore the swamp both on his own and with fellow investigators, he eventually formed the Bridgewater Triangle Expedition Team (BTET). The group organized formal searches and, just as importantly, collected stories from others, which were disseminated by way of a postal newsletter. One of the reports published in this manner involved a woman who allegedly saw a "bear-like animal" eating a pumpkin in her garden on the outskirts of the swamp.[16] The animal stood upright on two legs like a human. When it heard the woman, the creature turned around and looked at her with reddish-orange eyes before it ran into the woods clutching the half-eaten pumpkin in its hand.

A similar creature, possibly the same one, was spotted by a member of DeAndrade's own research team in 1985 as they huddled around a campfire one night. Mike Foster said he was tending to the fire when he noticed a "tall furry man-like animal" standing about forty-five feet away.[17] It had reddish-orange eyes that were illuminated in the darkness. After a few moments, it ran into the woods. A police officer told DeAndrade he also saw a "tall furry man-like creature" run into the woods near Raynham around the same time period.[18]

Shortly after DeAndrade's own sighting, another sighting was reported by local trapper and West Bridgewater resident, John Baker, who said he encountered a hairy, ape-like thing in the swamp during the early 1980s. It was the dead of winter and Baker was navigating the Hockomock River late one night running trap lines for muskrat. As he worked the lines from his canoe, he began to feel as though someone or some*thing* was watching him.

"Something was following me and I knew it was big," Baker told a reporter at the *Boston Herald*.[19] "So I took the boat down a small creek to a dry hill and it kept moving." As he paddled quietly, he could hear its footfalls crunching in the thin covering of ice along the bank. When Baker finally stopped, a "shadowy, hair-covered giant" walked into view a few yards away.

"I knew it wasn't a human because when it passed by me I could smell it," Baker continued. "It smelled like skunk—musty and dirty."

Baker had been working the swamp for more than thirty years and was used to the cold night air of the bottomlands. But what he saw that night chilled him far worse. "My heart was up in my throat," he confessed. "I don't know what it was, but I know I saw it and it was out there."

Just prior to Baker's encounter, a smaller ape-like creature was reported only a few miles to the south at Lake Nippenicket, or "The Nip" as locals call it. The Nip is the largest area of open water associated with the swamp, prized not only for its productive fishing but for its air of primitive nature. In 1980, Mark St. Louis and Peter Blumberg were paddling its waters when they caught sight of a small orangutan-like animal sitting on the shore of a small island.[20] Curious, they paddled their canoe to the beach and tried to get a better look. As they did, the creature fled into the trees. They got out of their boat and attempted to chase it, but it was nowhere to be found. It would seem the immensity of Hockomock's terrain and the depths of its shadows are in favor of that which populates its legends.

Shadows in the Sky

Hockomock's legends are not simply confined to its shadowy grounds. Sometimes they can be found soaring above it. Such is the case for a series of very unusual bird sightings that occurred in roughly the same time frame as many of its hairy hominoid reports.

The earliest of these dates back to 1971. That year, local police officer Thomas Downey was driving west of the swamp when he caught site of a huge bird flying above the trees. It appeared to be something extremely unusual with an estimated twelve-foot wingspan, black feathers, and a raptor-like beak. He only observed it for a brief period before it was out of sight, but felt certain that whatever it was, it was not typical of the local wildlife. Whether as a result of his sighting or by odd coincidence, the location where the sighting occurred has become known as "Bird Hill."

In 1984 a witness reportedly saw not one but two monstrous birds flying over the Hockomock. In this case the witness described them as looking "prehistoric." The birds were black in color and appeared to be fighting as they flew.[21]

Two years later, Kathleen Garner of West Bridgewater had a much closer sighting. She was driving with her husband along a residential street when a huge bird swooped down and nearly collided with their windshield. "I screamed and it took off," she told a reporter from *The Enterprise* newspaper.[22] Garner described the bird as being at least six feet in height with a wingspan of eight feet or more. It also had a beak full of teeth! This is an interesting detail since no modern birds have teeth. (Aside from a few avian species such as the goose, who have something resembling pseudoteeth, the last toothed birds died out in the Pleistocene epoch around 2.5 million years ago.)

A short time later, two men were walking along a dirt road in the swamp when they discovered what appeared to be tracks of a huge bird. In a report submitted to DeAndrade, one of the witnesses (Jim R.) described the impressions as being "the size of a grown man's hand." They were pressed about one inch into the soil and had indications of large talons.[23] As the men were examining the unusual tracks, the bird suddenly appeared overhead.

"It had a wrinkled black face, dark black feathers, and long brown legs which dangled behind it," the witness wrote. "I would guess the wingspan was a bit over six feet." The men watched until it disappeared behind the trees. They were convinced it was not a normal bird of any kind.

Another witness was driving near a cemetery in West Bridgewater when something even more bizarre flew over the car. It had a wingspan of approximately ten to twelve feet and looked more like a *humanoid with wings* than it did a bird.[24] Needless to say, the witness was stunned.

In addition to Hockomock's mystery birds, unexplained lights and crafts have continued to make appearances over the years. In one case, witnesses reported seeing strange-moving orbs hovering along the railroad track near Raynham. Even more astounding, multiple witnesses saw a bizarre flying craft above the Raynham Dog Track in 1979. Two of these were WHDH Radio reporters, Steve Sbraccia and Jerry Lopes, who were driving to the dog track one evening when they noticed a bright light moving above the treeline. As it got closer, they pulled over to get a better view.

"I remember saying to Jerry, 'What is that over there?'" Sbraccia recalled in a 2013 interview.[25] "So we pulled his vehicle over and all of a sudden the stars blotted out in the shape of an arrow as this thing passed overhead." It was huge, perhaps larger than a football field, and shaped somewhat like a baseball home plate with a pointed front end. It had a series of reddish lights around its perimeter and a brighter, white light mounted at the front. Sparks appeared to be falling from it.

As the two men watched, the craft moved directly overhead as it passed them. The night was clear, so they had an excellent view. According to Lopes, "It just hovered there for a minute, and the next thing you know, it just took off."

Sbraccia and Lopes kept their sighting quiet for a time until the same object was reported by others. Once the newspaper picked up on the story and printed it, the two reporters decided to come forward and provide the details of their own sighting. No one, including the authorities, had an explanation. It remains one of the best examples of a UFO sighting on record and one more notch in the notorious belt of the Hockomock.

The Widening Gyre

Of all the creatures said to haunt the Hockomock, perhaps none is more perplexing and oddly chilling than the one encountered by Bill Russo on a lonely autumn night in 1990. At the time, even though he lived in Raynham just a few hundred yards from the edge of the swamp, Russo had never heard of the Bridgewater Triangle or thought much of Hockomock's legends.[i] But he would soon be beckoned into its swirling vortex by an unlikely siren.

According to Russo, that night he came home from work as usual and prepared to walk his dog, Samantha.[26] Russo worked the evening shift, so it was after midnight when he and Sammy set out for their nightly exercise and fresh air. They normally walked

i The area of the "Bridgewater Triangle" was defined and named by cryptozoologist and author, Loren Coleman, in the 1970s.

along the sidewalks toward town, but on this occasion Russo decided to take a more scenic route, which would take them along a power highline through the woods.

After about half a mile, they came to a road that meets up with the highline. A lone streetlight provided a bluish circle of light, but the rest of the area remained shrouded in darkness. Suddenly, the dog began to tremble and pull on her leash. As Russo tried to calm his companion, he began to hear what sounded like a strange voice. It was repeating "Eee wah chu, eee wah chu," over and over.

Russo looked around trying to determine the source of the strange voice, but saw nothing. Samantha still cowered as the voice became louder. Finally, something emerged from the darkness.

"Into the circle walked a hairy creature about three to four feet tall, which weighed probably a hundred pounds," explained Russo. "The creature stood very straight on two feet and looked at me with eyes that were too large for its head—like the eyes of an owl."

The creature was covered in "coarse, unkempt hair" and had a distended potbelly. Though it was small, Russo had the impression it was somewhat old.

Russo stood motionless as the creature continued to repeat "eee wah chu, eee wah chu" in a crude voice, occasionally adding the phrase "keer keer." Then it began motioning with its arm. It seemed to be beckoning Russo to come closer.

Neither Russo nor Sammy was willing to advance. There was something ominously frightening about the entity, despite its small stature. "We stood watching the thing for not more than a minute but it felt like hours," he recalled. "It kept speaking to us, but made no further movement toward us."

Russo summoned the courage to ask it a few questions, but it only responded with the same repetitive phrase: "eee wah chu... keer keer."

Thoroughly frightened, Russo began to back away as Sammy followed. They turned and walked home as fast as they could, occasionally glancing back to see if the thing was in pursuit. It was perhaps the longest walk of his life.

When he arrived home, Russo couldn't sleep. He stayed up all night replaying the incident in his head over and over, trying to figure out what the creature was and what it wanted. Finally, something clicked.

"My best guess at a translation is this," Russo said. "It was speaking English and saying, 'We want you. We want you. Come here.'"

The thought was absolutely chilling.

While the strange being and its actions seem uniquely odd, its presence doesn't seem too out of place in terms of long-standing folklore in the region. What Russo didn't know at the time is that the Bridgewater Triangle area is said to be the home of the "Pukwudgie," a race of goblin-like creatures whose description is very much like the thing Russo encountered.

The origins of the Pukwudgie can be traced back to the Algonquians, and in particular the Wampanoag tribe who once inhabited the area. According to the Wampanoags, Pukwudgies were "capricious and dangerous creatures who may play harmless tricks or even help a human neighbor, but [were] just as likely to steal children or commit deadly acts of sabotage."[27] They were described as standing 2-3 feet tall with grayish skin, long ears, and protruding bellies. The name Pukwudgie (and its alternate spellings) roughly translates to "person of the wilderness" in the Algonquian language.

Early Native tales portrayed these creatures as sort of whimsical and magical. They were mischievous, but not really harmful. As time progressed, however, the Indians began to view the creatures as deceitful and evil. It was believed they would go so far as to abduct humans or even kill humans by pushing them off cliffs or attacking them with small knives or poisonous arrows.

As with most magical creatures in Native American folklore, Pukwudgies are seemingly nothing more than mythological tricksters that populate their fictional stories. Yet in modern times more than a few people wandering the areas of the Freetown Forest and Hockomock Swamp claim to have spotted entities that bear an eerie resemblance to these legendary Algonquian goblins. This includes Russo, who ironically had never heard of the Wampanoag's tales prior to his encounter. Only later did he learn of the similarity, which not only casts a chilling coincidence upon the whole affair, but gives the Pukwudgie a prominent place within Hockomock's modern menagerie.

The true nature of Hockomock's sinister side may well be locked in the same shadowed realms as that which haunts the fringes of our own reality: animals that have yet to be identified or hybrids which have risen from the peat-bogged backwaters. These monstrosities are as mysterious as the apparitions that take on the ghostly forms of Native Americans or souls lost forever in the swamp.

Students of the paranormal have suggested the swamp's curious nature can be traced back to the blood spilled upon its ancient ground. The region has certainly seen its share of human atrocities brought on by the colonial forces who sought to rid the area of the Algonquian people during King Philip's War. The area in which Hockomock is located was one of the largest concentrations of colonial presence and warfare that eradicated the original inhabitants in a manner that surely cast their living energy into the very ground where they died. As their blood blended with the boggy backwaters, perhaps the swamp and the surrounding triangle were cursed in a way we may never understand.

The rugged terrain of the Hockomock
(Photo by Dave McCullough)

2

GREAT DISMAL

It would be hard to find another place in North America whose name conjures a more haunting visual image than our next swamp: the Great Dismal. Just the mere mention of its ominous, gloomy moniker evokes a somber mental picture that speaks volumes without ever having set foot there.

While the name Great Dismal may sound like the fabricated setting of a creepy horror novel, it is indeed a real place with a fascinating undercurrent of purported ghostly encounters, phantom lights, and swamp monsters that would rival those of any fictional creation. The swamp was given its official name by the eighteenth-century planter, Colonel William Byrd II, who first surveyed the area in 1728. Like others, Byrd found the place to be rather "dismal," noting that he and his party were "almost devoured by yellow flies, chiggers and ticks" before getting lost and running out of food.[28] Author Hubert Davis offers a more sinister interpretation of the name, noting the French translation *marais maudit* which literally means "cursed swamp."

Cursed or not, the swamp is certainly "great" in terms of size. The Great Dismal is one of America's largest swamps, originally comprised of over one million acres sprawled across southeastern Virginia and northeastern North Carolina along America's Eastern Seaboard. While its size has diminished over the years due to encroaching development, it still covers some 750 square miles, which includes an interior lake and a 107,000 acre wildlife reserve in addition to the endless expanse of forested wetlands. This primitive world is home to a wide variety of trees, plants, wildlife, and a solemn air of mystery that rolls like a thick fog from its secluded backwaters.

The Algonquian tribes who originally inhabited the area were the first to speak of its mysterious dark side. They told of a "great fire bird" who lived at the heart of the swamp.[29] Its eyes burned like flames, and it would singe the top of the trees with its smoldering wings as it flew. The bird was known to swoop down and snatch children or even warriors whom it carried back to its nest to be devoured. The nest, they said, was constructed from the tendons of its victims, while skulls and bones littered the ground around it. Legend declares the nest was eventually flooded, and this created Lake Drummond, a near circular body of water located in the center of the swamp. To this day, scientists themselves are still puzzled as to how the lake was actually formed. Some suggest it may have been a meteor, yet there's no evidence of a meteor on the bottom.

The Chesapeake and Chowan tribes told of a ghostly spirit who inhabits the dreary shores of Lake Drummond. Known as the "Lady of the Lake," the spirit was supposedly that of an Indian maiden who died an untimely death a few days before she was to be married.[30] On certain nights thereafter, she could be seen paddling her white canoe across its placid waters with a firefly lamp illuminating the way.

This tragic Native American story went on to inspire two famous poems: Edgar Allan Poe's "The Lake" and Thomas Moore's "A Ballad: The Lake of the Dismal Swamp." Moore, who visited the swamp in 1803 before the drainage canal into Chesapeake Bay was completed, overheard the legend while in nearby Norfolk, Virginia.[31] He penned his eloquent poem while at a tavern there. After its publication, the poem was so popular it sparked a tourism boom for the area.

Poe published his legend-inspired poem in 1827. His version was more symbolic with a prose full of contrasting dark imagery, danger, and delight.

Then–ah then I would awake
To the terror of the lone lake.
Yet that terror was not fright,
But a tremulous delight–

- excerpt from *The Lake. To–* by Edgar Allan Poe

Stories of malevolent witches were also woven into early Native legends. One particular witch lived deep within the swamp's shrouded canebrakes. When hunters would pass through, she would turn herself into a deer and taunt them by running just ahead of them. She would lead the hunting party and their dogs deeper into the maze of blackwater until they nearly died from exhaustion.[32]

Her wicked ways finally came to end when a clever Indian guide used the Devil's own magic against her. According to the legend, the guide was leading an old hunter through the swamp when they came upon the witch in her human form. Startled, the old crone quickly transformed herself into a deer and bounded away.

The hunter and his guide immediately gave chase with their dogs (as hunters always did). But instead of falling for the witch's cruel game, the Native guide managed to direct her into a heavy bog filled with briars and brambles. When she became trapped, she transformed herself into a tree stump just as she leapt away from the dogs. The guide then called upon the Devil, who quickly arrived on the scene bringing with him a powder made of dried bear liver, dried toads, and ground-up rattlesnake rattles. The guide sprinkled the ingredients around the stump—which looked like a deer in mid-leap—and a fiery flame quickly erupted. The guide danced and chanted around the fiery stump as lightening flashed overhead. By doing this he sealed the witch's fate, forever trapping her in the form of the tree stump.

A tree stump which looked like a fleeting deer was indeed present in the Great Dismal Swamp, seen by various people throughout the years. Later, however, it was destroyed when a fire swept through the swamp. But the witch's tale has never been forgotten.

Since the days of Native legends and prominent poets, the Great Dismal Swamp has continued to hold its fascination while building a reputation as a place of modern paranormal activity. Along with the tradition of ghostly inhabitants and witches come sightings of strange lights, creepy canines, ape-like creatures, and even an entity that sounds eerily similar to a werewolf. Within its thick maze of cypress, juniper, and black gums, it is said no one can hear you scream.

Creepy Canids

One of the earliest modern tales of intrigue dates back to 1902 when locals near Suffolk, Virginia, were terrorized by a beast they called the "Dismal Swamp Monster." According to an article from the *Richmond Dispatch* newspaper, the creature first made its presence known when it killed seven dogs owned by Edward Smith.[33] It apparently ate two of them before it attacked Smith himself. Two weeks later, the beast was encountered by a local merchant, Frank Ames, who shot at it several times before urging his own dogs to pursue. The dogs merely cowered in terror as the thing made its escape. Later, it was seen prowling around a nearby water well.

The creature, as such, was described as having a wolf-like appearance with a "long, gaunt form, vicious eyes, and shaggy, yellow hair." Its eyes, they said, shone at night with a "phosphorescent glow."[34] Rumors that it was actually an escaped lion or tiger made the rounds; however, most of the townsfolk—including the eyewitnesses—stood by the inclination it was some sort of unusual animal. Fearing for their livestock and even their own lives, they promptly organized a hunting party to flush the creature out. During one of the hunts, some of the men located what they believed to be the culprit in a stable where they thrust their guns "through knot holes or cracks in the planks and fired a volley at him with deadly effect." After examining the corpse, it was discovered they had killed a large mastiff dog which belonged to a foreign traveler. Authorities seemed pacified by this victory, although a domesticated dog seems to be an unlikely candidate for a "dog-eating beast." The debate, however, is moot, since the newspapers went silent following this incident, leaving the rest to conjecture.

In recent times, reports of dog-like beasts in and around the Dismal take on a much more frightening mien. On one occasion a boy was lying in his bed after dark when something approached his window.[35] He lived with his mother in a small, wood-frame house at the edge of the swamp in Camden County, Virginia, so it was not uncommon for wild animals to prowl around. However, this was no normal animal. According to the report, as the boy gazed out his window, the creature suddenly rose up on its hind legs and looked in. The thing had reddish-brown, matted fur and a face that looked like a cross between a wolf and a human. Its snout was very much wolf-like, yet the rest of its facial features were "very human" with high jaw bones and eyes that seemed more human than animal. Spittle ran down its face as it looked directly at the boy.

Terrified, the boy crawled out of his bed and ran to his mother's room, where he stayed the rest of the night. The next morning, he and his mother went outside to examine the ground in front of his bedroom window. They noticed the dirt was "stirred up" as if something had been walking around. They also noticed scratches in the wood under the window where paint was missing. Had the thing been trying to get in? It was a horrifying thought.

FLEE FROM SWAMP MONSTER.

Virginia Terror Kills Seven Dogs and Eats Two.

Special Dispatch to The Inter Ocean.

SUFFOLK, Va., Feb. 14.—L. Frank Ames, merchant of Bennett's Creek, thirteen miles from Suffolk, last night had an experience with the Dismal Swamp monster which earlier this week killed seven of Edward Smith's dogs, ate two of them, and attacked Smith himself.

Ames shot the thing several times without effect, and urged his six dogs to make an attack. The dogs fled in terror and hid. The monster escaped unharmed, and was seen later sitting complacently on the curbing of Henry Jordan's well.

Superstitious persons are much upset over the strange visitation, and farmers are alarmed about the safety of their stock. It is described as of long, gaunt form, vicious eyes, and shaggy yellow hair.

One of several newspaper articles about the Dismal Swamp Monster (Chicago Tribune – February 15, 1902)

Man-Like Monsters

In addition to dog-men, Bigfoot-like creatures have also been reported in and around the Great Dismal. In 1982, John Cartwright was hunting in Pasquotank County, North Carolina, near Elizabeth City and the Great Dismal when he saw something that shook him to the core. It was October and he'd agreed to accompany his friend and his friend's father on a deer-hunting trip. Cartwright was not much of an outdoorsman but figured it would be a nice gesture to join his friend, who was an avid deer hunter. The location of the hunt was on their private property about one-half mile from the closest road. They had some old cabins there, which were elevated on stilts in case the swamp became flooded. The men drove to the cabins the night before so they could be in their deer stands bright and early.

At about 5:00 a.m. the next morning, the men proceeded to the hunting location. Cartwright was placed in one stand while the other two men went on to other stands. As Cartwright sat back enjoying the crisp morning, he saw several bear and deer moving about but didn't have the heart to shoot one. At around 9:00 a.m., however, the pleasant morning took a turn.

The first thing Cartwright noticed was a horrible odor. "It smelled worse than a dog that had been playing in a sewer," he reported. "Then I heard it before I saw it, snapping twigs as it walked."[36]

Cartwright's first thought was that his friend might returning to get him. But then he noticed a dark figure in the woods ahead. It was large and man-like and appeared to be covered in hair.

"It looked to be about eight foot tall, and just unbelievably massive in the chest and shoulder areas," he said. "Its fur was very dark black in color. I only caught a glimpse of its face, as its back was to me, and it looked hairy except around the eyes. The neck was short and stubby with a kind of furry ridge that ran up the back of the neck, to the top of what looked like a slightly pointed head that sloped down to the forehead, like a gorilla."

The thing stood there for at least five minutes eating leaves. Its human-like hands seemed to carefully select the ones it wanted. This gave Cartwright plenty of time to consider what it could be. He'd just seen bears, and he was absolutely sure this was not one. It looked far more ape-like.

Eventually the creature turned and headed back into the woods. Cartwright could hear it for several more minutes as it cracked noisily through the trees. "Needless to say I was so scared I almost peed myself waiting quietly for my friends to come save me," he confessed. "When they arrived, I told them the story, and of course they thought it was a bear."

Cartwright knew better but decided not to press the issue. He may have been a first-time hunter, but he knew the difference between human, bear, and something far more unusual.

Just one year prior, my good friend, author David Weatherly, was exploring the swamp with two fellow researchers when they saw what might have been the very same creature! At the time, the guys were researching one of the Dismal's famous "witch tales" and were attempting to locate the witch's actual house (rumored to be haunted). After trekking deep into the swamp, they finally located the home, which was essentially a creepy-looking, rundown shack.

The group explored the structure and the surrounding grounds until daylight started to fade. David was adept at navigating the swamp (which was close to his home at the time) but even so, he did not want to get lost there in the dark. It was far too dangerous. So he and his associates set out at a fast pace, trying their best to avoid pitfalls as they made their way back with limited visibility. Their flashlight had been inadvertently broken when one of the guys set their pack down in the witch's house, but luckily the night sky provided sufficient illumination.

"The sun had gone down fast, but the moon came up," David told me. "It was full, or close to it, so there was at least some moonlight to assist on the trek. I would typically move for a bit, then stop and check my bearings, using any kind of landmarks that were there."

The group made good time and finally came to a spot where the trail veered off sharply and opened into an oval-shaped clearing. David recognized the spot and knew they were on the right course. He walked to the center of the clearing and looked around to get his bearings. As he did, his eyes focused on a pair of trees about twenty feet away. For a moment they looked normal, but then he noticed something odd.

"The tree on the left seemed like a normal cypress, but the

one on the right was chopped off, only going up around seven or eight feet," he explained. "Not only that—once I fully focused on it, I realized it was very broad, and following the image to the ground, I saw two separate trunks."

As he continued to focus on them, David realized the tree on the right was not a tree at all. It was something alive, and it moved! As the three men watched, the top part of the "tree" turned slightly, causing the moonlight to reflect a reddish-orange eyeshine. The thing then made a loud huffing noise and lowered its arm as it stepped to the side. It had been holding onto the tree beside it.

"It was now very clear this was a large creature standing on two legs looking in our direction," David continued. "While it seemed a long moment, my logical mind tells me it was only a few seconds before it turned around completely and walked away from us."

The stunned group stood silent, trying to process what they had just seen. David noted the swamp had also gone strangely silent, with no insects, night birds, or frogs bellowing in the bottoms as they should have. It was eerie and unnatural.

When the guys finally resumed their trek out of the swamp, they said nothing to each other. David locked the details in his mind, knowing full well they'd encountered something that few others would ever see. It was a chilling experience he would never forget.

More than a decade later, in 1994, Ray Johnson was walking along a trail through the thick undergrowth on the northeast end of the swamp when he had a similar experience. Johnson had spent the evening deer hunting and was finally making his way out of the swamp at dark. Though the deer were plentiful, he hadn't had any luck. Save for a small fox walking by his stand, things had been unusually quiet.

As Ray followed the bobbing beam of his headlamp, he

breathed in the cool, moist air. It was early November, but not yet cold enough to require his heaviest jacket. It was perfect weather for hunting, and Ray was in his favorite place to do just that. The rugged swampland was tranquil and remote. His wife, however, never liked him going there especially in the evening. She said it had a reputation of being haunted. That sort of thing only amused Ray. In hindsight, perhaps he should have listened to her.

"I stepped over a fallen log and suddenly I saw a figure come out of the trees to my right about thirty yards ahead," Johnson told me in an interview. "It walked on two legs to the middle of the trail and stopped and turned towards me."

Johnson froze in his tracks. The sudden appearance of the figure startled him. At first he thought it was another hunter. However, the figure was not carrying a rifle or a bow, nor did it seem to be wearing any clothes. Its body appeared to be covered in short hair. Johnson felt a wave of fear shoot through him. Whatever this thing was, it stood about seven feet tall and was apparently not human.

As the hunter watched in disbelief, the creature turned its head slightly as if it were deciding what to do. "I wanted to just run, but my feet wouldn't move," Johnson explained. "It was like I was frozen."

A split second later, the thing turned and darted into the trees on the opposite side of the trail. Johnson could hear its heavy footsteps as it bounded into the tangled undergrowth. It was enough to convince his own legs to run. Adrenaline pumping, he took off as fast as he could. As he passed the spot where the thing had stood moments before, he didn't dare stop to look. He just wanted to get back to the safety of his truck. He could still hear branches breaking. The noise seemed to be moving away at first, but then started to get louder, as if the thing was heading back his direction. Johnson ran even faster, nearly dropping his gun as he stumbled. When he finally got to his truck, he quickly opened the door and jumped in. His heart was pounding as he started it up and sped away.

"I'm not going to say I know for sure what that thing was, but I know it wasn't a man or a bear," Johnson concluded. "Whatever it was, it really scared me."

Needless to say, Johnson no longer wanted to hunt in the swamp.

Spectral Spirits

When it comes to ghostly happenings in the Dismal Swamp, they are not confined to Native American legends. There's still the occasional report of a spectral white figure seen moving across the waters of Lake Drummond, suggesting that perhaps the fabled Lady of the Lake is still cursed by her lonely endeavor. Another spirit seems to be tied to an old hotel that once stood on the banks of the lake. This curiously located establishment, known as the Lake Drummond Hotel (or "Halfway House"), was an impressive yet unsavory sort of place constructed in 1829. It was a known hangout for fugitives and underage couples because the state line literally ran down one of its hallways. One could simply walk a few feet and be in another jurisdiction if one happened to be at odds with the law. The hotel was also remote and only accessible by traveling down a ten-mile stretch of logging road that ran alongside the Jericho Ditch.

According to the story, a traveling couple arrived at the hotel late one night.[37] He was a gentleman, and she was a common lady who seemed to be hopelessly in love with her suitor. The hotel was quite full, so the desk clerk assigned them to Room 6. The room was not often used, because for some strange reason, more visitors tended to check into it than ever checked out. The couple didn't care and excused the rather dusty conditions and cobwebs that filled the corners of the untended room. They were tired and fell quickly into a deep sleep.

Later the next day, the couple joined other guests in the anteroom. The woman was rather quiet, clinging to the arm of her man, while he was gregarious and outgoing. As he sampled glasses of the local swamp spirits, he began to speak of curious legends involving pirates and thieves who once came to the swamp. Perhaps he believed they had hidden their treasures there.

The woman grew tired and eventually returned to their room, while the man continued to talk to guests far into the evening. The more he talked and drank, the more he seemed to lose his sensibilities. Finally, he simply got up and ventured out of the hotel and disappeared into the darkness as if he was on an important quest. Later, when his girlfriend returned to the anteroom, she was distraught to find him gone.

In the days and months that passed, the man did not return, so the woman continued to reside in Room 6. Each night she would walk onto the porch (which overlooked the swamp) and await her lover's return. But it never happened. Despondent and weary, she eventually died in her bizarre and lonely state.

From then on guests reported seeing a woman's ghostly figure haunting the porch as if she was still there pining for her man who never returned from the swamp. Even after the hotel was torn down, travelers in the area reported sightings of a ghostly white figure standing on the banks of the lake where the hotel had once stood.

Whether the tale is true or not, the mysterious Lake Drummond is definitely a focal point for much of Dismal's ghostly history. In another case, a young woman who lived in a village on White Marsh Road was betrothed to a young man who also went missing in the swamp.[38] On the morning of their wedding day, he went into the swamp to hunt so they would have venison for a feast. When he hadn't returned by evening, the men of the village prepared to go search for him. Desiring to search for him herself, the young woman convinced them to wait a bit longer. As they enjoyed drinks and food at the lonely wedding dinner, she secretly slipped off into the swampy woods to search on her own. Not surprisingly, she, too, was never seen again.

After their disappearance, the townsfolk theorized they had met up and simply chosen to live in some secluded spot of the swamp. It was more likely, however, that they perished after becoming lost in the foggy thickets. Perhaps this was confirmed by a strange sighting which occurred several years later. A man identified as Mister Crochet was staying at the Lake Drummond Hotel and walked onto the porch one morning. As he gazed across the serene lake, he was astonished to see what appeared to be a beautiful young woman in a wedding dress emerge from a thicket of reeds and bamboo. The location seemed far too impenetrable by anyone, much less a woman dressed like that. Crochet watched as she walked out onto a log about twenty feet into the lake and began to fish with a pole she was carrying. It was the strangest thing he'd ever seen. For several more days he observed her repeat the same pattern as if she were a spectral image trapped in time.

Similar phantom figures have been encountered at other locations in the swamp, typically on the old logging roads or near the network of drainage ditches. These appear to be ghosts of the past, dressed in either colonial-era clothing, vintage lumberjack outfits,[39] or slave attire. The Dismal Swamp was once home to thousands of fugitive slaves who used its ominous seclusion for safety. In fact, from about 1680 up to the Civil War, the swamp's communities were dominated by African Americans.[40] As a result, much of its folklore and odd ghostly reports involve former slaves.

For example, one prominent tale involves a hunter who encounters a ghostly slave guide. According to the hunter, he was out hunting with several friends when he got separated and became lost.[41] His compass would not work correctly, so by dark he was starting to panic. At that point he began to hear what sounded like footsteps moving through the swamp around him. He hoped it was his friends, but when a lone figure stepped out of the bushes, he could tell it was not. It appeared to be a black man dressed in tattered clothing without shoes. The black man stared with a hostile look.

A chill ran up the hunter's spine as he locked eyes with the strange man. An instant later, the man's angry look turned to one of compassion. He then looked to his right and faded away as if he were made of mist.

Now the hunter could hear a distant noise in the direction where the phantom slave had looked. He decided to follow the sound and in a short time came upon a fire road. As he walked the road, he could hear voices that became more distinct as he went. Finally, he came upon his friends, who had been desperately searching for him. It seemed the phantom had somehow directed him to his rescue.

Elsewhere in the morass, mysterious lights can be seen floating in the woods or hovering over flooded bogs. When eyewitnesses try to approach the lights, they either move further away or disappear completely, leaving the witnesses to wonder just what it was they'd seen. Some have dismissed this as an illusion caused by fox fire. Fox fire is a bioluminescent fungus like a mushroom that feeds on rotting logs. As it breaks down and consumes the wood, the resulting chemical reaction gives off an eerie, blue-green glow. The light can be significantly bright, enough to read by in the dark.

The glowing fungus was often referred to as "fairy fire" or "will-o-the-wisp" in past centuries, accounting for many a fabled tale and strange theory. We now understand this phenomenon to be the result of hispidin, a fungal metabolite that creates two enzymes needed for bioluminescence.[42] The only problem with using this natural occurrence as an explanation for moving orbs of light is that fungus does not move.

One of the strangest tales regarding the Dismal's dead involves a mysterious, vanishing graveyard. Over the years several visitors have allegedly stumbled upon this somber cemetery after becoming lost or disoriented. A man named John Sweet seems to have been the first to come across it.[43] During the depression years of the 1930s, he had taken a job working on one of the swamp canals being constructed near Portsmouth, Virginia. One afternoon as he was walking from the canal back to the camp where he lived with his wife, he came across an open area among the dreary trees. Within the clearing he noticed a group of grave markers that were old and weathered. Upon inspection, he found they were the gravesites of a family who must have lived in the swamp long ago. It seemed like something of historical importance, so John took a mental note of the location and hurried back to the camp to tell his wife.

On his next day off, John brought his wife to the location of the old graveyard. However, when they arrived John was dismayed to find it was not there. He was sure he was in the very same clearing, but no signs of the grave markers could be found. It was as if he'd seen an illusion, a spectral image of graves instead of ghosts. The couple became spooked and quickly left. Over the next year John periodically returned to the site, but never saw the ghostly graves again.

Reports of the vanishing graveyard continued to circulate in the area as others also said they had come across an isolated group of graves in the middle of the swamp that seemed to disappear. In some instances, the people could not locate them at a later date, and in other instances the markers literally disappeared when the witnesses looked away for a moment. Many times these witnesses were lost, and after stumbling upon the graves they somehow regained their orientation and found their way out of the swamp. Perhaps the spirits of the dead family were looking out for lost travelers whose lives depended on finding their way out.

Disorientation can be an alarming and sometimes deadly issue for those who trek the Dismal Swamp. One can easily lose their sense of direction due to the uniformity of the landscape. And even when the traveler is carrying a compass, it can still be a problem since compasses have been known to malfunction while in the swamp. In some cases it points in the wrong direction, and in others it spins wildly, leaving the traveler confused and ultimately lost.

The phenomenon may be tied to the paranormal or simply the result of magnetic fields that are thought to be hidden under the deep layers of peat. Whatever the cause, it has the potential to turn an exhilarating hike into serious fight for survival if one were to become lost in the deepest recesses of the Dismal's knotted quagmire.

"Washington at Lake Drummond Dismal Swamp"
(Courtesy of the State Archives of North Carolina Raleigh, NC)

The Darker Side

While it's not uncommon for swamps to be associated with things of a darker nature, the Great Dismal seems to have more than its fair share of things like witches, cannibal witches, and dead bodies. Tales of witches in particular date back to the earliest inhabitants, who believed shape-shifting entities were present among them. In some cases these were mischievous yet harmless witch-women who could transform from human form to that of a woodland creature, such as a deer. While in this form they would taunt hunters as they were pursued through the mire, often resulting in the hunters getting lost. Sometimes these playful witches would simply assume the form of a doe in order to eat from their neighbor's crops.

Other stories are not so playful in that superstition and strange circumstances resulted in deadly action. In one such story, a couple who built their cottage on one of the swamp's many small islands had trouble scratching a living from the bog.[44] When the husband suddenly died from presumably natural causes, the widow became a hermit. Perhaps it was the horrible, shocked look upon his death face that caused her to withdraw. Within a short time, her once beautiful demeanor took on the ravages of age as her face became wrinkled and shriveled, her teeth blackened, and her hair transformed to gray straw. The locals felt pity, even when a round of disease began to take their livestock. But that was short-lived. Soon people also began to die of unknown causes, stamped with the very same look of horror upon their faces as the widow's husband. One unlucky resident described visions of terrifying things which appeared on the walls and ceiling of the room as she breathed her last breath. At the moment she expired, someone noticed a cat-like creature with satin-black skin lurking just outside in the moonlight. Several men ran out the door and pursued it through the woods, where it finally ended up at the widow's island cottage. They were shocked to find the hermit woman sitting in front of a fire, chanting in a strange tongue.

Superstitions ran wild, so the locals brought the woman to trial and found her guilty of witchcraft. The sentence was death by burning at the stake. On the night of the planned execution, it is said, the entire community turned out to watch. The suspected witch was tied to the stake and the fire was set ablaze. However, before she was burned, one of the men took pity on her and cut one hand free so she was not in total discomfort. In that moment she pulled forth a strange ball and cast it into the air. It flew into the darkness, where suddenly she made her escape by following a string that fell behind it. The crowd gasped as the witch screeched into the woods, never to be seen again.

Not to be outdone, another ghastly tale involves a witch who rivals the child-eating crone of Hansel and Gretel fame. The story begins with a man named "Jack" who lived in the small village of Currituck.[45] He often hiked into the depths of the Great Dismal, where he enjoyed the solitude of its rich landscape. On one occasion, however, a plume of black clouds moved overhead in the late afternoon, causing him to become disoriented. Soon, he was lost in the brambles and blackwater as he tried to regain his sense of direction amid a cacophony of eerie howls.

Jack was just about to give up and succumb to the hopelessness of his situation when he noticed a sliver of light piercing the dense thicket in front of him. He walked toward it, hopeful that it was a way out. When he got close enough, Jack could see a small, rickety shack in the middle of a clearing. An old woman sat on the porch, creaking back and forth in a wooden rocking chair. She appeared to be eating something, perhaps a pie.

Relieved, Jack walked across the field toward the dwelling. The woman promptly greeted him with a smile revealing a mouthful of rotted teeth. No matter, she seemed warm and friendly, and offered Jack some goat's milk and a chair upon which to sit.

As Jack and the woman chatted, he drank the milk. Within a short time he began to feel sleepy and the woman invited him to lie down on a bed inside the shack. Before he drifted off, he noticed the woman was starting a fire under a huge metal pot suspended within a large fireplace.

When Jack finally awoke, he found himself bound tight with a rope. He heard the old woman cackle as she loomed above him with a rusty knife. Years later, only the sawed bones of his body could be found. The flesh had presumably been boiled and eaten by the grim, cannibalistic witch.

The reality of this story, like the others, is suspect, since Jack couldn't have conveyed the details if he had been eaten by a witch! Regardless, the swamp has been the site of bizarre murders and lost bodies that can be confirmed. On November 22, 1987, a man was walking along the Dismal Swamp Canal near the Virginia-North Carolina border when he saw what appeared to be the body of a woman at the bottom of the steep, rocky embankment. He called police, who later identified the victim as Kathy Bonney.

According to investigators, Kathy's body was thrown into the swamp after being shot multiple times. The investigation into the apparent murder took several strange twists before police eventually determined Kathy had been killed by her own father, Thomas Lee Bonney. After several rounds of questioning, Bonney finally admitted to the act, telling police he and his daughter had been arguing in his car before he shot her and dumped her into the canal.

During the trial, Bonney's defense lawyers contended their client suffered from a multiple personality disorder and that "an evil personality" named "Demian" was in control of his mind when his daughter was shot.[46] Bonney himself insisted his daughter was still alive and she had even visited him one night at the jail. During one of the videotaped interrogations, Bonney foamed at the mouth as he screamed out: "You're just a mortal. You don't know anything!"

Possessed or not, Bonney was found guilty of first-degree murder.

Not far from where Kathy Bonney's body was dumped, another murder victim was found on May 31, 2015. In this case, the victim, later determined to be a Virginia Beach woman named Brianna Armstrong, had been killed and dismembered before being thrown into a wooded area surrounding the Great Dismal Canal in Chesapeake. Evidence at the scene led police to a coworker who confessed to killing Armstrong. He was sentenced to a cozy forty years in prison.[47]

The gruesome reality of these acts, or even the premise of the tall tales, is by no means a reflection of the swamp itself. The Great Dismal is, in fact, a place of astonishing beauty. It's only that such places, especially this one, are shrouded in the deepest shadows of our strange, terrestrial world. Its very nature offers solitude, concealment, and endless mystery. Perhaps somewhere at the heart of this gloomy, fog-laden paradise lies the truth behind our darkest secrets, worst fears, and most primitive thoughts.

3

HONEY ISLAND

Just a few miles east of New Orleans, Louisiana, in the summer of 1963, two hunters were walking through the wilds of Honey Island Swamp when they came upon something that would forever change the reputation of this rugged patch of coastal lowland. The hunters, Harlan Ford and Billy Mills, said they were headed toward one of their hunting camps north of the Bradley Slough when they spotted a massive, hairy creature crouched on all fours with its back to them. At first they thought it was a wild hog, but then it stood up on two legs and turned around. This was no ordinary animal.

According to Ford, the thing was approximately seven feet tall with slender legs and a broad chest. Its body was covered in a layer of shorter gray hair, while longer hair grew from its head. Its two large, amber-colored eyes focused intently on the two men as they stood frozen.

Ford and Mills were only able to study the creature for a few seconds before it bolted into the trees. They immediately took off after it, but the creature easily outpaced them and disappeared into the long shadows of the swamp. After a few minutes they gave up the pursuit. The men were bewildered and rattled by what they'd seen. Little did they know, the incident would become the cornerstone of a legend that has become one of the Bayou State's most famous—that of the Honey Island Swamp Monster.

Though Honey Island Swamp is located less than an hour's drive from New Orleans' celebrated Bourbon Street, it could not be further from the festive lights and colorful beads. Here, the land is primitive and wild with a massive backdrop of swampy marshes, hardwood bottomlands, and river systems. It lies between the Pearl River on the east, West Pearl River on the west, and Lake Borgne on the south. To this day it remains one of America's least developed and most pristine swampland habitats, covering nearly 140 square miles.[48]

Honey Island was given its delicious-sounding name because of the abundant honeybees seen on its islands, yet bees are probably the last thing people think about these days when walking or boating its backwoods. Sure there's an amazing array of scenic beauty and wildlife there, but the story of the notorious monster has become so well-known in the area, it's bound to cross one's mind (if not their peripheral vision) as soon as the sun starts to set.

Sightings of a hairy, man-like creature in the area are thought to date back at least a century. Natives referred to it as "Letiche," while the Cajuns called it the "Tainted Keitre" or "La Bête Noire" (the black thing).[49] In modern times, the sighting by Ford and Mills in 1963 is considered to be one of the first, although they did not report it at the time. It wasn't until the story was featured on a 1978 episode of the television show *In Search Of...* that it became widely known.

According to Ford's granddaughter, Dana Holyfield, who has written extensively on the subject of the monster, her grandfather was employed as an FAA Air Traffic Controller at the time and also had a pilot's license for small aircraft.[50] On the weekends he loved to spend his time outdoors, often hunting or fishing deep in the swamp. He was a man who knew his way around every crook of Honey Island and was very knowledgeable about the types of animals that lived there.

In the years following their encounter, Ford and Mills kept the details mostly to themselves while keeping a close eye on the swamp in case the creature reappeared. Despite their vigilance, however, they didn't see anything else until 1974, when Ford and his son Perry were duck hunting in the swamp. In the course of the hunt they came upon two dead boars lying near the water with their throats slashed and their bodies mangled. Blood was trickling from the neck of one boar into the water. It appeared something strong and massive had taken them out. Alligators would have been a good candidate, but gators typically drag their prey into the water, not maim and leave bodies. The hunters were perplexed until they discovered a set of strange footprints nearby that had three large, clawed toes and a smaller dewclaw. Harlan immediately thought of the animal he'd encountered a decade before.

According to Ford, he did not have plaster at the time, so he returned later to cast several of the impressions—which appeared to be from more than one animal based on differences in size. Now armed with evidence, Ford phoned the Game Warden at the Louisiana Wildlife Commission and told him of his experiences. The warden examined the tracks and agreed they did not match any known animal. They were also evaluated by Louisiana State Naturalist George Stevens, who concluded the creature must weigh upward of four hundred pounds.[51]

The story of the tracks and Ford's seminal sighting were featured in "The Swamp Monster" episode of *In Search of...*, along with stories by another local who claimed to have seen the resident monster. Ted Williams—an experienced trapper who had lived in the area all of his life—said he'd seen the creature many times prior to 1978, and in some cases, a pair of them together. According to Williams, the beast was approximately seven feet tall and covered in gray hair with long arms—just as Ford and Mills described. Williams said he'd even seen the creatures swimming as a human would.

Williams's claims are interesting, especially in regard to the aquatic behavior, but unfortunately a follow-up interview is not possible. Williams took his boat deep into the swamp one day and never returned. To this day no one knows what happened to him.

In 1973, one year prior to Ford and Mills's discovery of

the alleged tracks, the Louisiana news service reported that a local swamp guide had seen a mysterious man-like entity in the swamp. Greg Faulkner, a student who also conducted guided boat tours, said he was boating down a bayou channel when he "rolled over" something that caused his outboard motor to kick up.

"I stopped and looked," Faulkner told reporters, "but I kept going up the bayou."[52] When he happened to look back, he saw a man-like animal come out of the water and walk up onto the bank. He described it as being about five feet tall and black, although he couldn't tell if it had hair or skin due to it being wet. "It was running on two legs," the guide explained. "It ran up on the bank and disappeared."

Faulkner quickly turned the boat around and motored back to the spot where the thing had emerged from the water. There he found a set of "fairly large tracks with five webbed toes." Whatever this thing was, it seemed very well adapted to the watery environment.

Even further back in 1960, Dudley Clark and three of his friends were hunting in Ponchatoula about thirty miles from Honey Island Swamp when they saw a "giant, hairy ape-looking thing in the woods far away from any houses." This was three years prior to the sighting by Ford and Mills, which up until now has been considered the first report.

I found out about this incident when I came across Louisiana musician Kenneth Clark, who said his father may have been the first to see the alleged creature. According to Kenneth, his father (Dudley) was spooked by the sighting, since it was like nothing he or his friends had ever seen or heard about. The hunters watched it for a few moments until it caught sight of them and ran off deeper into the woods. When they examined the area where the thing had been standing, they found three-toed footprints. The whole incident was very strange, his father said.

Girl and the Gorilla

During the time I was researching this subject, I was fortunate to have been also contacted by another early eyewitness whose account had never been made public. The witness, Dez Crawford, had apparently seen a strange animal near Honey Island Swamp in 1967—still years before the legend was widely known.

During a personal interview, Crawford told me that when she was a child, her dad and uncle would regularly take their families camping and fishing in the Honey Island Swamp area. They lived in New Orleans and enjoyed the outdoors, so the location was perfect for weekend getaways.

On this particular weekend, they loaded the families into two big cars and headed to a campsite along the Pearl River. There were eight kids, including Dez, along with their parents. After the adults and older kids had set up the tents and a pop-up camper, they spent the rest of the day playing, fishing, and catching frogs as they usually did. By suppertime they had caught enough for a big fish dinner, which they enjoyed by the fire.

"It was just starting to get toward sunset," Crawford explained. "My younger girl cousin and I both needed to urinate, so we ventured further into the bushes than the boys so they would not tease us."

The girls each found a spot and went about their business. Crawford finished up and was just about to rejoin her cousin when she noticed a peculiar, hairy animal standing a short distance away. It was looking directly at her, as if watching curiously.

"I looked up, and at a distance of about the width of our front yard at home, on the other side of a small clearing, I saw what I thought was a scruffy gorilla standing there," Crawford said. "It was getting dusky, and the sun was getting low, but I could still see very clearly. It stood erect, arms down at its side, leaning slightly at an angle in a curious posture. Its face was neutral—no bare teeth or grimacing; just an impassive expression—but it was very focused. For some reason I thought it was a "girl gorilla" because the chest had two soft-looking protrusions, more like breasts than pectorals."

Crawford was both concerned and astonished as she watched the creature, trying to figure out what it was. Although her first impression was "gorilla," she knew that wasn't quite right, since gorillas were normally black. This thing had reddish fur, like an orangutan, yet she was sure it was not that type of ape either. She stood transfixed, as did the animal, for several moments.

"There was a noise from camp, and the spell was broken," Crawford continued. "Then it turned around and quickly walked into the woods. It didn't make any noise; it didn't run; it was just *fast.*"

Crawford grabbed her cousin and they ran back to camp with Crawford shouting that there was "a gorilla in the woods." The adults were skeptical but couldn't deny the fact that Crawford was visibly shaken. She had obviously seen something.

The men grabbed a shotgun from the car and had young Dez show them where she'd seen the "gorilla." After looking around they sent her back to camp and went searching through the brush. A short time later they returned without having seen anything. "They came back concerned and were convinced that I had seen a bear," Crawford recalled.

As an adult, Crawford still remembers the incident clearly. It made such an impression on her at the time, not only because she was convinced it was not a bear, but because she was the kind of kid who loved and studied all sorts of animals.

"I much preferred playing outdoors than playing games of make-believe," she said of her childhood. "I was reading well above my grade level, and I was fascinated by animals. I read books about animals and could identify a great many local animals, birds, and fish by the time I was six."

She described the creature as being about as tall as a "door," in her childhood estimation, with "a smooth face and light-colored eyes, no neck, no snout, and no visible ears." It resembled a primate, but did not seem as apish as one would expect. At the time she could only believe it had escaped from a zoo. She had never heard of Bigfoot, much less the Honey Island Swamp Monster. Although this incident took place four years after Ford and Mills claimed they saw something in 1963, their account would not be made public for another decade. Whatever Crawford saw was not influenced by a preconceived notion of a swamp monster.

I spoke with Crawford on quite a few occasions and found her to be credible, well-spoken, and very detail-oriented. I wondered why she had never come forward with the story prior to her sharing with me (and my late colleague Dr. John Bindernagel), but I already knew the reason. Like other witnesses who saw strange things back in those days, she suffered ridicule. When she shared the story with friends, no one believed her, and on some occasions she was even made fun of. So naturally she stopped talking about it all those years ago and only confided in a few people such as her husband.

In the end, I appreciated her coming to me with the account. Even if she was young at the time, I have no doubt she saw what she said she saw. The fact that her account has never been made public before now makes it all the more intriguing.

The Legend Grows

Once the story of the Honey Island Swamp Monster was disseminated in the 1970s, other reports began to creep out of the swamp's shadows. One of these reports was made by Herman Broom. Broom said he was in the swamp near Lateral Canal (close to the location of Ford's initial sighting) when he came upon a hairy beast with a man-like face. The creature lingered a few moments before retreating into the woods. He and several others pursued it but never saw it again.

Another came from witnesses living in Perlington, Mississippi, on the east side of the Pearl River near Honey Island Swamp. Deonka Bridgewater said that in 1975 she was awakened by her neighbor's dog one night. They were barking furiously, so she and her siblings got out of bed to see what the commotion was.

"Looking down from our window we saw something in the garden" she explained. "There was only natural light, but the thing was only about twenty or thirty feet away. It was squatting down eating the vegetables. I could even hear it eating from where I stood."[53]

The thing was built like a human, yet it was much more animal-like with "dark, shaggy brown hair." Once they realized what they were seeing, the children began to scream. When it heard the sound, the thing looked up at them but continued eating.

"I remember that, by its mannerism, it had no fear of us what-so-ever and made no attempt to leave the area or hide in any way," Bridgewater continued. "I can't say exactly how big it was, but I know it was bigger than the average person. When it looked up at us … its eyes glowed white in the darkness."

The commotion eventually woke up their grandfather. When he saw the thing, he quickly grabbed his gun, ran outside, and fired it into the air. Bridgewater said they watched from the window in horror as the thing stood up and ran on two legs toward the river. It ran unbelievably fast. The following morning, the family ventured outside to inspect the garden. There they found "very large human-like footprints" in the soil.

"I had never seen anything like that before and never have since," Bridgewater concluded.

Five years later, on the Louisiana side of the Pearl River, two hunters were approaching the bank on a cloudy, misty morning when they heard a loud splash.[54] They turned to see a dark-haired, muscular creature standing with its back to them on the river's edge. It was about seventy-five yards ahead. They watched as it pulled a cypress stump from the mud and threw it into the river.

The hunters were completely dumbstruck by the sight. Surely they couldn't be seeing such a creature. But they were, and within a few more seconds it saw them too. It must have either sensed or smelled the men, because it turned and looked directly at them before walking briskly away down the river. When it looked at them, they could see its face was hairless around the nose and mouth area, much like an ape. The thing appeared to be about six or seven feet tall, stood upright, and looked very heavy.

After they felt it was safe, the hunters walked to the area where the man-thing had been standing. There they found "large human-like footprints, much larger than a man's print." Judging from other cypress stumps in the vicinity, the creature must have been very strong to have picked one up and thrown it any considerable distance into the water. Needless to say, the men left the area as fast as they could.

During one of my own visits to Honey Island Swamp, I spoke to Dan Holyfield (Dana's father), who told me of a strange experience he had in the late 1980s. Dan said he'd been turkey hunting one evening and was returning to his home by boat along the Pearl River. Just about the time the sun set, he hit something in the water that caused his engine to sputter out. A few seconds later he caught sight of something swimming away from the boat. When it reached the shore, it crawled out and stood up on two legs. It was hard to see in the dim twilight, but it appeared to be wearing a dark covering of some kind as it shook off the water and loped toward the woods. Dan called out, asking if he was okay, but the figure only glanced back a moment before it faded into the darkness.

"I thought it might be a person I hit with my boat," he

told me. "But I don't know why a person would be out there swimming like that."

Puzzled but still under the assumption it was an injured person, Dan maneuvered his boat to the shore where he scanned for blood with a small flashlight. No blood was visible, however, there were three-toed tracks that looked very much like those Ford cast in 1974. Dan got out of his boat and cautiously followed the trackway but never located the strange, bipedal figure.

The connection to the water and the action of swimming seems to be prominent in many of the reports. Not to mention, Dan's experience is eerily similar to the one reported by the swamp guide in 1973. In a similar case, Jason Holburn was at a place called Debbie's Ditch one night during a bright, full moon when he and an unnamed person noticed something walking on two legs across a canal approximately fifty yards away.[55] When it reached the other side, it shook the water from its hair and walked into the woods.

Moving Shadows

While the majority of strangeness in Honey Island Swamp seems to involve a large, hairy man-like creature, there are reports of other shadowy creatures, particularly black panthers. Panthers are, of course, real animals, but in terms of the "black" variety of North American wildcat, they technically do not exist.

The term "black panther" can be confusing since it doesn't necessarily refer to a distinct species of cat, but rather to any black (melanistic) specimens of any genus of large cat. For example, black panthers in Latin America are actually black jaguars (*Panthera onca*), and in Asia or Africa they are black leopards (*Panthera pardus*). In North America, however, the term black panther generally refers to black cougars (*Puma concolor*). The problem here is that no specimen of cougar has ever been proven to have this variant. The cougar, also known as a mountain lion or puma, is always tan or gray in color with a lighter underbelly. Rumored sightings of presumed black cougars have circulated in North America for at least a century, but as of yet, these shadowy felines remain unconfirmed and wholly classified as cryptids.

My first indication of a black panther phenomenon in Honey Island Swamp came when I checked into a motel in the area prior to an excursion into the swamp. While checking in I struck up a conversation with Bud Westmore, the motel's manager, which naturally led to some discussion about the Honey Island Swamp Monster. Westmore had an interest in the subject, but did not know anyone who had ever seen the alleged creature. However, he did tell me that he and several others had seen a huge, black cat roaming the woods of the Pearl River Wildlife Management Area.

Westmore told me his sighting occurred one evening in 2010 while he was deer hunting with his son. They were sitting in a tree stand near Peach Lake Cutoff as the day was just starting to succumb to dusk. The woods had been usually quiet, and Westmore didn't have much hope that the deer would move in before dark. Just before he decided to call it quits and climb down, he glanced out of the deer stand one last time. Something caught his eye. At first it looked like a moving shadow, but after a moment he realized it was a huge, black cat.

Westmore nudged his son, and they both watched as the cat moved silently along the edge of a small clearing next to the woodline. It was dark black in color and was much larger than any domestic cat he'd ever seen. Its movements were fluid, almost ethereal, as it crept another twenty yards or so before it turned and vanished in the trees.

Westmore felt a chill run through his body. The predator was like a living shadow, silent and deadly. Even though he was armed, the thought of climbing down from the stand and walking through the woods at that moment was alarming, especially since he was with his young son.

Ultimately, the descending darkness only made the prospect worse, so Westmore made the decision to go ahead and leave. As they walked from the woods, he kept a wary eye out, although he knew no amount of vigilance would stop an animal like that from stalking them.

Westmore recalled the cat as being a uniformly solid black color with no appearance of muted spots, which suggests it could have been a melanistic cougar as opposed to a black leopard or jaguar. Even though jaguars have been known to inhabit several of America's southern states, they have never been known to roam Louisiana. If it were a black cougar, then Westmore saw something that is completely undocumented.

A few months later Westmore mentioned the incident to a game warden as they were discussing the hunting season. To Westmore's surprise, the warden said he'd also seen the creature. It was strictly off the record, but he had no doubt some sort of mysterious panther was residing there.

During my travels, I met another eyewitness who claimed he saw a "black panther" near Honey Island in the summer of 2015. Randy Lee told me he was driving into the game reserve one evening with his wife when a large female hog and her baby scrambled across the road in front of them. A few seconds later, a dark cat jump from the woods and ran across the road very quickly, presumably in pursuit of the hogs. He described it as being larger than a domestic cat and covered in sleek, black fur. Like a moving shadow, it was there one second and gone the next.

Elusive Evidence

When it comes to evidence for the swamp's most famous creature, the prospects are rather controversial. In addition to

Harlan Ford's track castings, film footage has also surfaced. Ford's wife said she discovered a reel of 8 mm film in her husband's personal items years after his death in 1980. The film, which was labeled "Honey Island Swamp Monster," contains a sequence in which a large, bipedal figure is seen walking through the woods. The film appears to have been shot from the vantage point of a tree stand with the subject approximately fifty yards away. During the sequence, the dark, presumably hairy man-like figure enters from the right side of the frame and walks toward the left side of the frame. It's partially obscured by shadows, trees, and undergrowth but undoubtedly looks like a Bigfoot. Could this be the infamous Honey Island Swamp Monster? If so, why would Ford not reveal his amazing evidence while he was alive?

As these type of "unknown creature" films go, it's one of the better examples. The film stock looks like legitimate 8 mm, and the creature's movements, while humanesque, don't raise an immediate red flag to suggest it's a hoax. There is a jump-cut edit at the beginning of the footage, which seems odd, but this could be the result of several factors such as accidentally hitting the record on/off button after the figure enters the frame. The figure is not clear enough to rule out a person in a costume, but conversely it is not clear enough to say it isn't.

Ford's granddaughter, Dana Holyfield, believes the footage to be authentic and theorizes that her grandfather decided not to release it in order to keep the world from converging on his beloved wilderness to capture or harvest the creature. Another explanation might be that it was some sort of test footage or an idea for a movie based on his experiences and was never meant to be considered as actual evidence.

Speculation aside, the creature in the footage looks more like a traditional Bigfoot and not the creature with slender legs, a broad chest, and gray hair initially described by Ford. In fact, during a 1970s interview with WVUE-TV in New Orleans, Ford himself stated he didn't believe the Honey Island Monster was "related in any way to the well-known Bigfoot, or the Fouke Monster [of Boggy Creek]." This opinion was presumably based on both its physical description and the anatomy of the tracks Ford claimed to have found in 1974.

Despite vague endorsements by the authorities, the nature of Ford's tracks and their authenticity has also been highly debated over the years. First, the three major toes appear to be long and finger-like with possible claws, which is not typical of Bigfoot tracks or even those of a known primate. There have been cases where regional Bigfoots appear to have three main toes (for example, the Fouke Monster), but the basic anatomy is still characteristic of a hominid. The Honey Island tracks, however, are more reminiscent of a reptilian creature with their alligator-like appearance.

In addition, a "fake shoe" was brought forth several years ago by a local resident who said he found it in the swamp. The shoe, which is fitted with a three-clawed "foot" identical to the famous track, was presented to two independent researchers from Mississippi who concluded it could have been used to create Harlan's famous tracks. Dana Holyfield looked into the matter herself and discovered the shoe size was smaller than her grandfather's foot. Without casting aspersions, she simply stated: "anyone can take an existing plaster track and make fake shoe-tracks to trek through the mud and claim it was a hoax." There are any number of speculations that can be made, but in the end the authenticity of the tracks and the film footage will remain a mystery now that Ford is no longer with us.

The monster, however, *is* still with us. Sporadic sightings of the creature continue to this day, with one of the most recent having been reported in 2012. In this case, a local woman said she was driving home from work not far from Honey Island Swamp when she saw a "large, hairy creature" cross the road.[56] She watched it climb over a gate and run into the woods. The Honey

Island Swamp Monster, it seems, is alive and well.

The wilds of Honey Island Swamp
(Photo by Lyle Blackburn)

4

OKEFENOKEE

In all my boggy travels, no place has impressed me as much by its sheer size as the Okefenokee Swamp. As I paddled its crooked canals, narrow channels, and briny backwaters, I couldn't help but marvel at the massive expanse of labyrinthine land that spread out for mile upon murky mile. It was a stark reminder of my relative insignificance within a primordial land where time seemed to have stood still.

I first explored the Okefenokee several years ago with my longtime research partner, Cindy Lee. We had previously visited several notable swamps in the southeastern United States, but this was the first time I can say we literally felt engulfed by a landscape that could have swallowed us whole if it so desired. Swamps are always dangerous, of course, but in this particular case Cindy and I were justified in our enhanced state of awe and trepidation, because just under the surface of this huge swamp lies the remains of everything from Native villages to airplanes that crashed within its borders, never to be found. If an airplane could disappear here, what hope could there be for two people and a small canoe should we encounter trouble?

As we paddled along in the late afternoon admiring the gently swaying cypress and sunlit islands, I thought of the strange tales I'd heard from Okefenokee over the years, which included monsters and lost planes. Cindy pointed out that we could have paddled right over the rusted hull of an aircraft or the submerged bones of its unfortunate passengers without even knowing it. The swamp is simply that big and that murky.

Okefenokee is located in south-central Georgia just north of the Florida border where it encompasses a staggering seven hundred square miles of rugged wetlands and wilderness. The swamp is noted for its massive floating islands of peat, which sustain enough vegetation that they're hardly distinguishable from solid land. When touched, the peat-moss islands are said to quiver, giving the Okefenokee its reputation as the "Land of the Trembling Earth." The word "Okefenokee" itself is derived from the Creek Indian word "oka-fenoke." which means "water-shaking."

On the whole, the Okefenokee is part of the Southeastern Conifer Forests ecoregion. Specifically, it's classified as a southern coastal plain nonriverine basin swamp and is the largest blackwater swamp in North America.[57] Its primeval appearance was formed by peat accumulation over thousands of years in a shallow basin along an ancient Atlantic coastal terrace, a geological relic of a Pleistocene estuary. The resulting expanse of boggy landscape covered by black gum, bald cypress, and swamp tupelo forests provides a home for throngs of massive alligators and snakes, along with panthers, bears, birds, turtles, and countless other creatures. Cindy and I once entered a large, marshy area peppered with peat islands where the echoing roar of bull alligators could be heard. It was impressive—and intimidating—to say the least.

On the subject of monsters, mysteries, and legends, Okefenokee certainly has its share. In a swamp of this caliber, how could it not? The mystery of the missing airplane is one such example. In the winter of 1943, a plane was flying over the swamp when something caused it to crash. Search parties were dispatched, but the swamp was just too formidable. According to the assistant director of the Fish and Wildlife Service in May 1944, no trace of the pilot or the crash was ever found.

Tragedies like this were not the first on record for the Okefenokee and any pilot familiar with the area was hesitant to fly over its expanse. "Pilots fly just as high as they're permitted to over Okefenokee," Charles Jackson of the Wildlife Service explained, "because they know if they crash, they'll never get out." He noted that compasses would do no good, and walking would be impossible. "You bog down at every step." And to top it off, the weight of the aircraft would eventually cause it to submerge, leaving any stranded pilot to face hungry gators with little or no protection.

According to one theory, Okefenokee may also have been the ill-fated last stop for the famous Flight 19. Known as the "Lost Squadron," this group of five navy torpedo bombers seemingly vanished into thin air during a routine training flight on December 5, 1945. The crew—which consisted of fourteen men—departed that afternoon from the Naval Air Station in Fort Lauderdale, Florida, and headed east to conduct bombing practice over the waters before it was supposed to head toward the Bahamas and then back to Fort Lauderdale. Somewhere along the way, however, the squadron encountered navigational difficulties. Radio conversations among the pilots, which were overheard by the base and other aircraft in the area, indicated they'd become lost. When asked what the trouble was, one of the pilots responded with the message: "Both of my compasses are out and I am trying to find Fort Lauderdale."[58] Sporadic contact between the pilots and others continued for an hour, but eventually ceased altogether as a result of deteriorating weather and/or other unknown factors. Neither the aircraft nor the crew was ever seen again.

Over the years, the case of Flight 19 has been examined by a number of military and aviation experts, as well as paranormal researchers who believe the disappearance may have something to do with the so-called Bermuda Triangle, an area east of Florida where unexplained disappearances have routinely occurred. This connection has created an inseparable link between the ill-fated flight and the Triangle, though it's not the only explanation that has been offered.

While the navy contends the pilots simply got lost and mistakenly flew northeast out to sea instead of west to Florida, others believe they were lost somewhere else. Among these is Gian

J. Quasar, an author who has investigated a range of mysterious subjects including the Bermuda Triangle and for which he is considered to be the foremost authority. In his book, *They Flew Into Oblivion*, Quasar lays out his belief that Flight 19 may have actually gone down in the wilds of Okefenokee while searching for Fort Lauderdale!

The basis of his theory originates from an aircraft report that confirms a naval carrier ship sighted four to six aircraft flying near Flagler Beach, Florida, at approximately 7:00 p.m. that fateful evening. Flagler Beach, he notes, is "exactly where Flight 19 should have come into the coast."[59] Later that night, the Air Transport Command (ATC) picked up five aircraft flying "near the Okefenokee Swamp in southern Georgia." The ATC had no record of any such scheduled flight in the area, and communication with them could not be established. According to Quasar, "Only Flight 19, limited to its training frequency (it was good only around Fort Lauderdale), would be unable to hear hails from the bases or be able to contact them." The mystery planes over Okefenokee never landed at any of the bases nor were they documented by any other sources that night. They simply vanished as if they had never existed.

While we may never know the truth behind the mysterious flight, if the crew did have to ditch in the swamp, the odds would not be in favor of the survivors—if there were any. The men, likely bleeding and injured, would have had to trek through miles of dangerous waters teeming with alligators and venomous snakes, not to mention bears or panthers, with no supplies or medical aid. We assume trained servicemen could survive such odds, but even healthy ones have been known to succumb to the swamp's treachery. In 1952 a pair of servicemen, William Denham (a seaman stationed at the Naval Air Station in Jacksonville, Florida) and Pfc. George Anderson rented a rowboat at Billy's Lake and set off to enjoy some paddling around Okefenokee.[60] After they failed to return, the National Wildlife Service launched a search, aided by a PBY airboat and an observation blimp from the Glynco Naval Base. It was to no avail. No trace of the men or their canoe was ever found.

Whether the crew of Flight 19 could survive or not, it seems ridiculous that five Avenger aircraft could crash in the middle of Georgia without anyone seeing it. But this is the Okefenokee. If there ever was a land to rival the mysterious allure of the Bermuda Triangle, this would be it.

Daughters of the Sun

Before the arrival of Europeans, southern Georgia was home to various factions of the Creek Indian Nation who revered the swamp as a place of beauty, fertility, and danger. Within the framework of their traditions, they told tales of witches, monsters, and enchanting spirits whom they believed inhabited the darkest depths of its labyrinthine forests. In one story, they told of a bottomless lake wherein dwelled a terrible, fire-breathing creature not unlike a dragon.[61] In another they spoke of an enchanted island populated by a tribe of incredibly beautiful maidens they called the "Daughters of the Sun."[62] These alluring women spoke in a harmonious, musical language and were thought to be the earthly equivalent of angels. The island, which they called "Lost Paradise," was said to have air so pure and waters so clean that flowers bloomed year-round. Its location was nearly impossible to find, however, since it was concealed by swirling mists and protected by alligator-filled lakes.

When the Spanish conquistadores arrived in the early sixteenth century, they made their way into the area as they searched for treasure and mystical places such as El Dorado. Upon meeting the native people of Okefenokee, they were intrigued by their tales, especially that of the lovely Daughters of the Sun. Fantasizing about what rewards the island and the maidens may hold for them, the greedy Spaniards tried to persuade the Indians to divulge the exact location. The Indians refused, however, even when threatened by the sword.

The conquistadores could not resist the allure of such a story, so they eventually set out on their own to search for the fabled paradise. Clad in their armor, the men trudged through the peat bogs like a brigade of metal soldiers. Nothing could have been less appropriate for the hazards posed by the swamp's interior. Within a short time, they returned from the swamp, exhausted and low on supplies. Without assistance from the Indians they would never find it, and the Indians would never betray the sanctity of their own secrets, regardless of whether they were accurate or not.

In the years to come, other Europeans made their way to the Okefenokee and were equally enthralled by the Natives' tale of the maidens and their mystical island. Like the conquistadores they were determined to find it, but in the end their searches always ended in failure, if not death.

According to the Creeks, on one occasion a group of their own hunters was pursuing game in the deeper reaches of the swamp when they became lost in the inextricable bog. The more they tried to find their way out, the more disoriented and dizzy they became until at last they were on the verge of death. As they lay dying, the angelic maidens suddenly appeared before them, offering fruit and other foods that restored their strength. The maidens then offered to escort the hunters back to the safety of their "own country," since it would be unwise to enter their village. The maidens warned that their husbands were fierce men and would not treat the intruders kindly.[63]

The Creek hunters were now able to see the fabled settlement, which was "situated on the elevated banks of an island, or promontory, in a beautiful lake." They tried to approach it, but were unable due to a perpetual labyrinth of bogs and marshes surrounding it. The closer they got, the further the settlement seemed, until at last they gave up and allowed the maidens to guide them out of the swamp.

When they returned home, the hunters told their tale to the tribe, confirming the mystical paradise did indeed exist. The story resulted in the other braves becoming so "inflamed with an irresistible desire," they sought to find the location again. However, all attempts failed. They could neither find the island nor even a pathway to it.

While tales of mysterious maidens and lost villages may seem like pure fantasy, a few historians have conjectured that in reality the Daughters of the Sun and their warrior husbands belonged to a lost race of Mayans who migrated to the region thousands of years prior. It's a stretch, but there's no doubt this American swampland could have provided just what they needed: adequate sustenance and ultimate seclusion. Seclusion that may also hide a race of huge, hairy giants.

The land overtakes an abandoned home in the Okefenokee (Photo by Lyle Blackburn)

Man Mountain

When it comes to tales of huge, hairy humanoids, Okefenokee does not disappoint in this category either. In fact, it's the setting for one of the earliest reports of a Sasquatch-like creature in the American South. According to an article in the *Milledgeville Statesman* newspaper, rumors of a hulking half man, half ape known as "Man Mountain" had long circulated in the soggy backwoods of the Okefenokee.[64] As white settlers began to move in—following several battles and treaties between expanding conquerors and indigenous peoples—they heard tales of this legendary swamp giant but were quick to dismiss it as superstitious folklore. That would change, however, in the summer of 1829, when two men and a boy decided to trek deeper into the heart of the swamp.

Taking advantage of an unusually dry season, they traversed for two weeks penetrating the interior until they came upon an ominous footprint so large it measured eighteen inches in length and nine inches in width with a toe-to-heel stride that easily stretched six feet. Thoughts of the Man Mountain immediately crossed their minds, resulting in a hasty retreat out of the swamp.

As word of their strange discovery began to spread among the locals, a group of nine hunters from Florida came forward and requested directions to the spot. They eventually made their way to the area where they discovered similar tracks, which they followed for several more days into the bog.

They finally set up camp on a ridge, hoping to refresh themselves before continuing further. As they were relaxing, however, a "wild beast" of some sort rushed out of the brush and advanced on them. Two of the men immediately fired upon it with their rifles, causing it to howl with a "deafening roar." The echo of the gunshots apparently aroused the maker of the giant footprints. According to the report: "The next minute he was full in their view, advancing upon them with a terrible look and a ferocious mien."

The hunters gathered in a close group and began to fire upon the hulking Man Mountain. They were finally able to drop the creature with a hail of bullets, but not before it ruthlessly killed five of their number by literally twisting their heads from their necks.

As the creature lay exhausted and dying, the four survivors "had [the] opportunity to examine the dreadful being as he lay extended on the earth, sometimes wallowing and roaring." It measured thirteen feet in length with its massive proportions complementing its towering height.

Fearing retaliation from any other "giants" living in the area, the men scooped up the remains of their comrades and fled from the swamp, leaving its carcass to rot. Presumably they told others of the incident, since the story was later related to the newspaper by a Mr. John Ostcan, who resided on the borders of the swamp in Ware County. The article concludes by saying: "The story of this report, as related above, is matter of fact, and the truth of it is accredited."

While the truth remains clouded in old newsprint and tall tales, it's curious to note that at least one man claims to have laid eyes on the remains of giants in modern-day Okefenokee. During the days when the Native Americans ruled the swamp, they built a number of earthen mounds in which they buried the corpses of their honored braves. One such mound was discovered on a prominent Okefenokee landmark known as Chesser Island. The island was owned by the Chesser family for many generations and subsequently bore their name. According to the *Atlanta Journal-Constitution Sunday Magazine*, Tom Chesser was working with a university professor in 1969 to excavate the mound when they uncovered thirteen complete skeletons.[65]

Chesser explained that: "Some of the skeletons were crossed, one on top of the other. Some were face down. All of them were perfect when they were first discovered. Teeth even still had some glaze on them, but when air struck, it crumbled them. *They were giants*. Those jawbones would go over my whole face."

Were these skeletons the remains of the fabled Man Mountain beasts? Or were they something else entirely? If the Man Mountain story is indeed true—or at least rooted in truth—then what were they?" Given its massive size and huge footprints, it does seem rather Bigfoot-like, although at no point does the source article say the being was covered in hair. If it was a bandit or feral human living in the swamp, then how could it be so large? If nothing else, perhaps the Man Mountain tale is merely an exaggerated version of a legend that continues to walk the Okefenokee.

Man-Apes and Pig-Men

Tales of brutish humanoids and ape-like creatures are not confined to the realm of Okefenokee legend. In modern times people have reported encounters with strange, hairy creatures who allegedly stalk the Land of the Trembling Earth. The creatures are often reported as "Bigfoot," although in local colloquialisms they are typically referred to as "Skunk Apes" or "Swamp Apes." The distinction between Bigfoot and these creatures is a bit fuzzy, but essentially Skunk Apes are thought to be a species of unknown ape that inhabit various regions of the southern United States, particularly Florida and the surrounding area. The creatures are said to reek of a terrible body odor (hence the name) and are often described as being smaller and more apish than the ubiquitous "Bigfoot."

The ape-like characteristics of these creatures are exemplified by a report from 1972. That summer a young man was camping with his family at Stephen Foster State Park on the west side of Okefenokee when he decided to explore the trails. As he was walking alongside a small canal, he began to hear footsteps behind him. He didn't think much of it, since it was likely one of his siblings following him. When the footsteps drew closer, he decided to hide behind a bush and surprise whomever it was.

"I figured they were going to scare me," he said in a report to the Georgia Swamp Ape Research Center (a group dedicated to the research of unknown hominoids in the area). "And I decided to let them sneak up and I would jump out and scare them."[66]

After waiting several moments, something did approach, but it wasn't one of his siblings. It was some kind of weird animal "like a cross between a chimpanzee and a little man." When it saw the teenager, it let out a bloodcurdling scream and then leaped at him.

"It knocked me down and tried to get its teeth in[to] my neck," the teenager recalled of the horrifying incident. He screamed as he wrestled with the animal, trying to keep its teeth from piercing his throat. A few seconds later he heard his parents shouting. They heard the screaming and were trying to locate their son. When the creature heard their shouts, "it raised up real slow and sniffed the air." Then it simply stood up, walked into the canal and swam to the other side, where it disappeared into the woods.

More recently, in April 2000, Lee Trowell and his father were boating along the western end of the Okefenokee Wildlife Refuge when they spotted a dike up ahead.[67] As the men approached, they saw a large creature jump up on the structure and began to walk across it on two legs. The thing was covered in light-brown hair and walked upright the entire time before it jumped down on the far side and ambled into the trees. They were stunned by the sighting, which took place in clear daylight conditions. They said it was not a man and definitely not a bear.

The creatures seem to utilize the canals, bridges, and other easy-to-travel pathways. In another report, two men claimed they were deer hunting near the Waycross side of the swamp when they observed an ape-like creature walking along a railroad track. The men described it as being approximately seven-and-a-half feet tall and covered in grayish-brown hair. When the creature caught sight of the hunters, it stopped and looked at them for several moments before it turned and headed deeper into the swamp.[68]

Another strange incident occurred on the banks of the St. Marys River, a tributary that originates in the eastern portion of the Okefenokee before it snakes along the Georgia-Florida border. The witness said he and a friend were taking a leisurely boat ride up the river in December 2012 when they struck something in the water near the Dunn Creek crossing. It was late in the afternoon and their cellphones had no service, so they were forced to paddle to an abandoned fishing camp where they could stay for the night.

The two men gathered wood and settled in for what they thought would be a peaceful evening around the campfire. At about 12:30 a.m., however, they heard something large moving through the woods down by the river's edge.

"We could tell it was moving towards us because the breaking branches and snapping twigs and crunching leaves were getting louder," the witness recalled. "When it got down to the river's edge across from us, we heard grunting and growling as well as stomping on the ground that was extremely loud."[69]

The witness decided to check it out, so he grabbed his flashlight and began scanning the opposite bank. "As I was shining, I could hear something moving through the brush towards me," he explained. "As it got directly across from me, I could see a shoulder and head." A few seconds later, a large, humanoid creature stepped out from behind a tree. The witness shined his light directly into its face. "When the light hit it in the face, it turned its head back to the direction it came from and took off," he continued. "It seemed mad [because] it started stomping and growling and breaking limbs again."

The witness returned to the campfire where his friend had remained, fearful of what might be lurking out there in the dark woods. They sat quietly and listened to the creature as it continued to make considerable noise in the woods for another hour. They could hear limbs breaking, knocks on wood (as if the creature were hitting the trees with a hard stick), grunting, and other unsettling sounds.

By the time daylight came, the men were ready to get off the river. They hurried into their boat and paddled until they came upon a Nassau County police boat. The officers on the boat arranged for them to be towed back to their launch point.

The witness said he felt a certain exhilaration by the strange encounter, but his friend did not feel the same. "I myself would love to return and search for the creature," he admitted. "My buddy, however … said he was frozen with fear and will never return there."

In some cases, even the folks whose relatives lived in and around the Okefenokee got their fair share of scares. Some years ago, a family was enjoying a bit of fishing at their grandmother's house when suddenly a creature emerged from the woods and grabbed their cache of fish that was secured on a stringer line in a creek. The witness, who was twelve at the time, recalled that his mother "began screaming and pointing at this thing that was carrying away our stringer."[70] The stringer was about thirty yards away, and they could clearly see some sort of bizarre hairy creature "loping along" as it tried to make off with the fish.

The witness's father shouted at the thing and began to run after it. When he got close it "turned around and screamed," giving the man second thoughts about what he was doing. At that point his father retreated, gathered the family, and left the area. According to the witness: "That night Granny informed the family she heard stuff around all the time but stayed in the house at night." It was sobering news to a boy who was not familiar with the haunting legends of the swamp.

In addition to Swamp/Skunk Apes, old-timers around the

Okefenokee also speak of something called the "Pig-Man." The creature's description is quite similar—with a hair-covered body, ability to walk upright, and a horrible smell—except that it's said to have a nose similar to a pig.

The possibility of such a bizarre creature definitely stokes my curiosity, but I'm uncertain whether this so-called Pig-Man is supposed to be a completely different creature or whether it's merely another term for the regional variety of Skunk Ape. The legend and terminology is undoubtedly tied to the Okefenokee Swamp, but when it comes to actual firsthand witnesses, I've never been able to track one down. That's not to say there isn't a particularly porcine ape prowling the swamp, however. Even though I haven't tracked down a firsthand witness in Georgia, I have received a few nose-raising reports from witnesses who swear they've encountered a monstrous-looking creature whose head is more like a pig than an ape. One of these occurred in 1973 near the state line between Arkansas and Oklahoma. The witness in this case told me "it was man-like with the head of a hog."

Porcine features aside, there does seem to be some sort of strange, ape-like creatures lurking in the Okefenokee. Take this last, chilling encounter as something to ponder: On October 7, 2009, a couple was driving south on US 441 just west of Okefenokee Swamp at about 11:30 p.m.[71] The night was draped in a heavy darkness, and they were the only car in sight on a very desolate part of the road. The woman (riding in the passenger seat) had just turned on the car's reading light so she could consult a map when the man (driving) noticed a "tall humanoid figure" standing on the shoulder. It was dark in color and was slightly turned toward the car's direction of travel.

"The figure was standing still, very vertically erect with both arms loosely down at its sides," the man reported. "The hair on the head was long and stringy, but the rest of the body hair seemed only two or three inches long and layed [sic] down rather than [stuck] out in a fuzzy fashion. It was lanky, rather than stocky, and was not crouching forward." The witness estimated its height to be around seven feet and its weight between two hundred and three hundred pounds. He could not make out any facial details, but the thing was very alive and very eerie in its appearance.

As they passed by, the man caught a whiff of a rank, musky odor that drifted into the car. He spotted some roadkill not far ahead, but it was fresh and not likely to have been the source of the odor. By the time the witness's wife looked up, they had passed the creature, but she did smell the rank stench. The witness said he momentarily considered turning around to investigate, but considering the remote location and the unsettling-looking animal, he decided against it. "I have hunting, camping, and Brazilian jungle experience and I am not easily frightened, but this shook me up," the man admitted. "I don't know what I saw but I will never stop my car at night anywhere in that area."

Spook Lights

As if bloodthirsty giants, rangy apes, and pig-men weren't enough, Okefenokee's legends are also stippled with tales of eerie lights and ghostly apparitions. One of these dates back to the 1930s when a man was allegedly fishing near the railroad tracks at Henson Creek. After a long day of fishing, he fell asleep with his head on the rail. A train suddenly appeared, but the man was so tired he was not roused by its roar. The train plowed ahead, beheading the poor fellow in the process. For years after the swampers claimed to see a headless ghost walking along the rails at night. It appeared to have a glowing lantern in its hand as it searched for its head. A man named Kevin Dial claims that his grandfather once saw the ghost. He described it as being solid white and six feet tall. As it approached, his grandfather was so frightened he actually fired his gun at it.[72] But as we all know, ghosts are impervious to bullets.

Other ghostly figures have been reported over the years, including those of Native American braves in full regalia. Like other swamps we've examined, the Okefenokee was the location of many bloody and tragic battles between indigenous peoples and invading outsiders. As the United States government began to seize control of Georgia in the late 1700s, the conflicts increased until Okefenokee became a battleground in the ongoing war between the US Army and the Seminole Nation (which included the Creeks). The conflicts continued until 1843 when the last of the peaceful Creek Indians were attacked along the eastern edge of the Okefenokee and the Altamaha River and marched at bayonet point to a fort in Alabama.[73] If tragedy gives rise to lingering spirits and angry ghosts, then this land is justified by their presence.

Strange lights continue to be seen. In one case, a witness said he was leaving his girlfriend's house on the outskirts of the swamp when he noticed a meteor shower. As he idled along slowly in his car trying to catch a glimpse of the celestial phenomenon, he noticed "a very bright white light about the size of a basketball and as bright as a vapor lamp flying through the pine trees ahead." It was moving quite rapidly about six feet off the ground.[74]

"I thought it was going to come out of the woods right on top of me and I hit my brakes," he said. "As soon as I hit my brakes … it immediately went back the way it had come." The quick reversal of the lights was odd and inconsistent with headlights or even a flashlight due to the speed. On a return visit, the witness had a better look around the area to determine if a car headlight or streetlight could have been the cause of the ghostly phenomenon. "I determined the woods were too thick and the highway and nearest streetlamp were much too far away," he explained. "I still don't know what it was that I saw, but it was very startling to say the least."

Some propose that swamp gas is the cause of such phenomena, but as of yet, these mysteries remain unsolved. There are things that we may yet understand or things that have yet to allow us to understand. Whatever it is that lurks in the enchanted Land of the Trembling Earth, it will continue to draw the curious into its primitive world of wonder. This, I must say, includes me.

Cypress trees in the Okefenokee Swamp
(Photo by Lyle Blackburn)

5

OTTINE

By definition, swamps are a type of wetland fed primarily by surface water inflow.[75] They can be categorized as *forested*, *shrub*, or *mangrove* (depending on the type of foliage present) and as *freshwater* or *saltwater* (depending on the water source). Freshwater swamps are primarily found inland, while saltwater swamps are located along coastal areas. In either case, these unique ecosystems are neither totally land nor totally water.[76]

All swamps form in areas of low elevation where water collects periodically or permanently. Saltwater swamps are specifically created when high tides cover low flats of mud and sand. Water-friendly plants such as mangrove trees begin to grow, eventually forming a thick base of roots. The roots, in turn, anchor the sand and sediments while their growth and decay promote the accumulation of soil. This condition eventually becomes a coastal swamp.

Freshwater swamps are typically formed in areas of low depression or around rivers and lakes as rain and seasonal flooding cause water levels to rise. The wet environment is then populated by water-tolerant vegetation, which helps maintain the delicate balance of moist, swampy conditions. Cypress and tupelo trees are the most prominent types of hardwood vegetation populating forested freshwater swamps. The knobby root systems of the cypress are perfectly suited for this type of ecosystem, thriving in the soaked conditions and providing stability and cover for a variety of animal species. Spanish moss often hangs from the branches, giving the swamp its age-old, spooky look.

Shrub swamps are similar to forested swamps except the landscape here is dominated by shrubby foliage instead of trees. Likewise, mangrove swamps are populated by the small, salt-tolerant mangrove trees and other plants that can flourish in the brackish, saline coastal waters.

Technically, a *swamp* is just one of four types of wetlands. The other three categories are *marshes*, *bogs*, and *fens*. Each of these has its own characteristics and subcategories. I've alternately referred to some of the swampy locations in this book as "bogs," although a bog is actually a separate type of freshwater wetland characterized by spongy peat deposits, evergreen trees, and a sphagnum moss floor. Fens are another variant covered by grasses, sedges, and reeds, while marshes are either coastal or inland areas periodically flooded with water and populated by herbaceous (nonwoody) vegetation.

In most cases the presence of a swamp only seems natural given the particular landscape conditions such as elevation and/or the presence of water. In places like Louisiana, for example, a bayou or swamp seems perfectly ordinary. There are, however, swamps that seem virtually out of place when compared to the surrounding elements. One such place is the intriguing Ottine Swamp of Texas. Although Texas is not the first state that comes to mind when thinking of swamps, it actually boasts upward of seven million acres of wetlands, making it one of the swampiest states in the country. Yet even in a state familiar with swamps, Ottine stands out as an anomaly.

Land of the Lost

Located in the south-central portion of the Lone Star State between Austin and San Antonio, the Ottine Swamp seems as alien to the region as a bagel at a southern BBQ. The majority of the surrounding landscape epitomizes the flat, sparsely treed Texas brushlands, yet the swamp is more befitting of something found further east along the Gulf Coast with its boggy grottos, lush dwarf palmettos, and gently swaying Spanish moss.

The reason this wetland seems so oddly placed is because it's a "relict ecosystem." This type of habitat (estimated to be at least twelve thousand years old in this case) has the ability to thrive in geographic isolation from its original, larger community.[77]

The conditions that resulted in the formation of the Ottine wetlands are a combination of periodic flooding of the San Marcos River and the output of an underground spring which forms the headwaters of the river. The swamp, which spans nearly two hundred acres, derives its name from the nearby small community of Ottine and is part of the greater Palmetto State Park.

Aside from the dwarf palmettos and ghostly moss, the swamp once contained a number of sulphur springs known regionally as "mud boils." The mud boils dried up in the 1970s, yet even today the place still oozes with a spooky, primordial atmosphere like a forgotten remnant of the Jurassic age. During daylight hours it would not seem surprising if a small dinosaur walked out of the thick palmettos or sloshed through a briny pond. As nightfall approaches, the swamp takes on a more sinister appearance as the pointed fronds of the alien plants crouch among shaded bogs of standing water.

Not surprisingly, Ottine is a place where legends simmer and sightings of a strange swamp creature have been reported. The creature is said to be a dark, black thing—a thing that can blend so well into the murky marsh that it's virtually invisible. Known locally as the "Ottine Swamp Thing" or simply "The Thing," this alleged cryptid falls somewhere between a Skunk Ape and something far more unexplainable.

Early reports of the Ottine Thing can be gleaned from the 1981 book, *Ghost Stories of Texas,* by Ed Syers. Within its pages Syers recounts a conversation with a man name named Berthold Jackson, who tells of his own experiences with the Thing of Ottine Swamp along with several secondhand stories.[78] Jackson—a Texas A&M University graduate engineer and skilled woodsman—

claims he encountered the creature in the swamp on three occasions. He described it as being something of an ape-like entity, black or gray in color, four to eight feet in height, one hundred pounds or more in weight, and extremely fast. Its footprints, he said, are "like a small woman's hand except it comes to a point at the base of the palm." It also has a chilling cry which he describes as "somewhere between human and animal." Jackson cannot provide further specifics on its anatomy, however, since he's never actually laid eyes on it. This, he says, is because the Thing has the ability to render itself invisible or at least camouflage itself so well that only its movements can be seen as it stalks through the brush.

On one occasion, Jackson says he and a friend were hunting in the swamp at night when the creature got between them. "We could see the brush move," he explained. They shined a carbide light directly at it, but could not see a thing; not even eyeshine. After it fled they discovered a significant number of snapped limbs, which confirmed something large had come through. Jackson goes on to relay several similar accounts, including one in which three men were running a trotline one night when the creature stalked them. "The thing came along the bank," Jackson recounted. "[T]hey could see those bloodweeds move as it followed."

Syers's book details other accounts of a similar nature. In each case the witnesses felt they were being stalked by a strange creature, but could never quite see it clearly in the blackness of the swamp. In other instances the creature was said to have scared campers and residents by grabbing car bumpers or shaking mobile homes in a violent manner. A number of these events took place at Lookout Hill near the entrance of the Palmetto State Park. Two young hunters, Brewster Short and Wayne Hodges, were preparing to return home after a hunting trip when something unseen reared up on the back of their car. It was scary enough to send them fleeing in haste, leaving their hunting dogs to fend for themselves.

Given the vague descriptions, apparent powers of invisibility, and secondhand nature of most reports, the question as to whether this is/was a real creature or merely a legend is a pertinent one. The ability to be "invisible" certainly pushes it toward the realm of legend or at least supernatural, yet Jackson's comparison to an "ape" brings up the possibility of a Bigfoot, perhaps one with an extraordinary knack for concealing itself among the palmettos. While South Central Texas would not be considered a prime Bigfoot habitat, the possibility that one of these creatures could travel through the swamp or the winding woods along the San Marcos River is not out of the question (if they do indeed exist). Regardless, with just a handful of secondhand reports and a description that tests the limits of even Bigfoot, the stories could be dismissed as mistaken identity or exaggeration if not for a couple whose more recent, chilling encounter suggests perhaps there is something out there that cannot be explained in simple terms.

The Tall, Black Something

In June 2014, Kristie Pustejovsky and her husband decided to do some hiking around Palmetto State Park. They had been there several times in the past and always enjoyed the peaceful trails that meandered from the park through the wilds of Ottine Swamp. This time, however, their hike would be far from peaceful.

"We were starting down the trail when we saw these weird footprints," Kristie told me after I got in touch by phone. "It had rained recently and there were these big footprints. They were a lot bigger than my husband's foot and they were shaped kind of funny."

The couple could not discern what had made the prints, so after some casual examination they continued down the trail which crosses the San Marcos River on the backside of the park. While looking around the riverbank, they were startled by several strange "howls" resonating from the surrounding woods. Like the footprints, they seemed odd.

"I grew up in the country around the river and woods, so I've heard coyotes and all that," Kristie explained. "But this was something we'd never heard before."

Undaunted, the couple proceeded back to the main trail and started walking toward Ottine Swamp. Within moments, a large rock landed on the ground behind them and tumbled down the hill. It was at least the size of a baseball. There didn't appear to be anyone else around, so they couldn't understand how it could have been launched into the air. By now they were feeling unnerved but decided there must be some reasonable explanation, so they forged ahead.

Kristie and her husband eventually entered the confines of the swamp, where dirt trails are interspersed with a number of wooden boardwalks spanning the low areas of brackish water. As they hiked along enjoying the rich landscape, they heard a loud crack behind them. They turned just in time to see a large limb land on the path where they'd just walked. The crash was followed by the sound of something running through the trees. When they looked up they caught sight of a dark, humanoid shape moving between the trees. It appeared to be running on two legs.

"I could clearly see the thing," she told me. "It was tall and black and very fast … faster than a person." Kristie was certain it wasn't a deer or hog, and it did not appear to be human. "I was watching it through the trees when it just disappeared, like it had stopped or something," she continued. "I was in shock."

The Pustejovskys focused on the spot where the thing had stopped. They could see what appeared to be some sort of "black thing either crouched or standing completely still beside a tree." While keeping their eyes on it, they examined the fallen limb. It was still green and not something that could have fallen on its own. They could only assume whatever had run away was responsible for making the limb fall.

By now they were frightened. Whatever was lurking there in Ottine Swamp seemed unnatural and menacing. Given the situation, they decided it would be best to proceed to the end of the trail as quickly as they could. As they walked, they kept an eye on the black thing which still appeared to standing or crouching in the distance. It remained visible until they had to cross behind some thick trees. When they reached the next opening, it was gone.

"Once we crossed onto the Ottine Swamp Trail, we heard the howl again, but close and clearer than before," Kristie recalled. After that they did not see or hear anything further. It was a day they will not soon forget. "It was the strangest thing I have ever seen in my life," she concluded.

As far as witnesses go, I found Kristie to be extremely credible and well-spoken. I had no doubt she and her husband experienced exactly what she described. The fact that she had not heard of the Ottine legend prior to the strange encounter is also significant. She told me that, in fact, she would have laughed at such a story prior to her own experience. Now she has a much different view.

Predators and Shadows

In my own travels, I've also been to Ottine Swamp and camped in the beautiful Palmetto State Park. During my visit to the park, I spoke to several caretakers and personnel working at the office. Unfortunately, none had heard of any recent sightings, but all were familiar with the tales and offered what general information they could.

The allure of the legend is certainly not lost on park officials. The gift shop stocks several Ottine Swamp Thing T-shirts and a souvenir cup with the same artwork. Along with the usual travel literature and maps, there's a photocopied article detailing the history of the creature (mostly taken from Syers's book). Of course I picked up a copy of the article and purchased one of the T-shirts. I asked the young girl at the front desk what she thought about the creature. She simply smiled.

A photo, taken by a camper on July 14, 2011, hangs on one of the walls in the park office. The photo shows part of a tree trunk in the foreground with green leaves and a glint of sunlight filling up the rest of the frame. A dark shape is visible next to the tree trunk. The shape is somewhat humanoid in form, although it has no definite arm or leg appendages. The caption asks, "Is this the Ottine Swamp Monster?" Perhaps, but there's no way to say for sure. The shape leads the brain in that direction, but it could just as well be a shadow, tree trunk, or even a reflection causing pareidolia (a psychological phenomenon that causes people to see patterns in a random stimulus). At the very least, it's interesting and reinforces the mystery that's haunted the grounds for all these years.

During my visit, I also learned that an Ottine Swamp Festival had been held in the past to raise funds for the Ottine Volunteer Fire Department and for Ottine Cemetery improvements. Small town festivals are not uncommon, but in this case the accompanying parade was led by none other than the "Ottine Swamp Monster." Not bad for a little-known legend.

After leaving the headquarters, I set up camp in the park before heading out to hike the swamp trail. Just as the Pustejovskys had, I proceeded out the back side of the park and crossed the bridge over the San Marcos River. I listened for strange howls as I went, but heard only the friendly tweeting and fluttering of birds. (The park is actually known for its bird-watching and is part of the Great Texas Coastal Birding Trail. Here you can find up to 240 different species, including eastern varieties such as the Kentucky warbler.)

I didn't hear any howls or see any rocks flying through the air, but the beauty of the river made up for it. The river here is wide and robust, flowing between banks populated by thick trees and striking foliage. If not for the bridge, it would have been extremely difficult to cross the water on foot.

After ascending the far bank, I walked until I reached a sign that signifies the beginning of the Ottine Swamp Trail. The vegetation here was noticeably different, growing more lush, green, and exotic. The swamp's unique ecosystem was evident even at its furthest boundaries.

As I entered the trail, I could see how the environment could easily evoke tales of strange inhabitants or conceal any large animals that may choose to pass through or take up residence. The landscape alternated with patches of lanky mesquites, thick grass, heavy brush, and root-twisted bogs. The presence of the diminutive palmettos made it all the more odd. I was used to seeing this type of fauna in places such as the Big Thicket of East Texas or more commonly in Florida, but it was completely bizarre in the middle of Texas. I felt as though I was on an elaborate movie set rather than in a real place.

The movie vibe is exactly why Texas filmmaker, Robert Rodriguez, chose to use the park for his 2010 *Predators* movie. Based on the original *Predator* movie from 1987 starring Arnold Schwarzenegger, Rodriguez's sequel takes place on an alien planet where a group of elite warriors is dropped off on a fictional planet to serve as worthy game (prey) for its alien residents known as "Predators." The majority of the movie was filmed in Hawaii—which served as the alien planet setting—while some scenes had to be shot closer to Rodriguez's studio based in Austin, Texas. Ottine Swamp was chosen as the perfect stand-in, doubling for the alien planet/Hawaii—quite a feat for Texas!

I didn't see any alien Predators, but around dusk I caught a glimpse of a dark shape in the high grass about sixty yards away.

At first I thought it was a rotting tree stump, but then it moved. I looked more closely and realized it was a feral hog. I noticed four others standing nearby, foraging in the muddy bottoms. After a few moments they caught my scent and bolted out of sight. While these were not apes or "monsters," it was a good example of how difficult it would be to see any dark-haired animal in those conditions. If the hog had never moved, I might have believed it was indeed a tree stump and simply walked on down the trail.

As darkness continued to envelop the boggy bottoms, the atmosphere seemed to grow darker with it. What was once a scenic walking trail became a whispering wood full of shadows, some that seemed to move. I forged ahead, relishing the spooky surroundings where eyes began to peer back as they caught glints from my flashlight beam. I heard a few heavy rustles in the brush but could not identify the source. For fun I let out a few random howls but got no response save for a chorus of frogs who paused long enough to entertain my silly antics. As I continued my hike, I couldn't help wondering if something unknown really could be lurking in the shaded bogs of Ottine's primeval world.

I eventually reached the end of the long, looping trail and made my way back toward camp in the darkness. A coyote howled in the distance, trying to rustle up the evening pack. They responded with howling yelps of their own.

Though I did not see any cryptids, monsters, or dinosaurs during my exploration, I thoroughly enjoyed camping and hiking along the beautifully maintained Ottine Swamp Trail. Its spooky tranquility not only offered a refreshing respite, it provided a rare glimpse into a primeval world of the past where the possibility of modern-day mysteries still exists.

The unique flora of the Ottine Swamp
(Photo by Lyle Blackburn)

6

ALTAMAHA

Within the vast countryside of eastern Georgia flows a waterway some have referred to as the "river that nobody knows." It's a wide, dark, and twisting body of water that cuts an unassuming path through miles of floodplain forests, swamps, salt marshes, and sparsely populated areas where natural ecosystems flourish in hidden domains. Though it may be overlooked by some, it's one of most important natural features along the southeastern coast, providing both a substantial river channel for drainage and a network of vast, swampy inlets and tributaries where abundant plants and wildlife flourish. This is the Altamaha River.

Located entirely within Georgia's boundaries, the Altamaha drains eastward from its origin at the confluence of the Oconee and Ocmulgee Rivers (near Lumber City) to the Atlantic Ocean near the small town of Darien. Its route covers more than 130 straight-line miles with a floodplain that engulfs approximately fourteen thousand square miles, making it one of the largest river swamp systems on the Atlantic coast.[79] Its massive volume, which pours 100,000 gallons of water into the ocean every second, ranks it as North America's third-largest contributor of fresh water to the Atlantic Ocean.[80]

Like many of America's natural resources, the Altamaha River basin has been affected by some amount of deforestation and encroachment, yet parts remain relatively untouched. Numerous national and state-managed wildlife refuges surround its banks and inlet islands, helping to preserve and protect both the river and its associated swamplands. These areas support a variety of unique fauna and flora, including Radford's mint (*Dicerandra radfordiana*), a rare mint known to grow only along the Altamaha

River sand ridge. The Altamaha basin was also the only known habitat for one of the most mysterious plant species ever found in North America, the Franklin tree (*Franklinia alatamaha*).[81] Known commonly as the lost camellia or Franklin tree, this genus of the tea family was discovered along the banks of the river in the mid-eighteenth century, although it has not been seen in the wild since 1803.

In addition to rare plants, more than 120 rare or endangered wildlife species can be found along the Altamaha. These include several rarely seen reptiles and amphibians, such as the bird-voiced tree frog, gopher frog, rainbow snake, and glossy crayfish snake, along with a host of typical denizens like salamanders, bullfrogs, alligators, and turtles. With its wild nature and ability to support such a vast diversity of species—both common and rare—the Altamaha River has often been called the "Little Amazon."

Given its vast expanse and reputation for hosting rare species, it's perhaps not surprising that the Altamaha is also associated with sightings of a mysterious, aquatic creature whose legend dates back to the coastal seafaring tales of yore. The creature, known as the Altamaha-ha or "Altie," has primarily been reported along the tributaries associated with Altamaha's coastal estuary in and around Darien. It has been described as something reminiscent of the Loch Ness Monster, although it's said to be more snake-like with a long, dark body mostly devoid of fins.

The first sighting of a possible unknown creature in the Altamaha waters was recorded by both the *Charleston Mercury* and the *Savannah Georgian* newspapers in April 1930. The witness was a trader by the name of Captain Delano, who often made runs between the towns of Charleston and Brunswick. Delano claimed that while he was sailing in his schooner, he saw a strange animal swimming near St. Simons Island below the mouth of the Altamaha. The reporter from the *Savannah Georgian*, who spoke to Delano personally, said he described it as "being about 70 feet long, and its circumference about that of a sugar hogshead, moving with its head (shaped like an Alligator's) about 8 feet out of the water."[82] (A hogshead is a large, wooden cask or barrel used to transport liquid or dry goods, such as sugar.)

Following Delano's sighting, several plantation owners on St. Simons Island reported seeing a huge, dark animal swimming in the same area on multiple occasions. They described it as being between forty and sixty feet long with the ability to roll over like a porpoise and spit or spew water into the air. It left a considerable wake behind as it swam, and on at least one occasion it was seen alongside a smaller creature, presumably an offspring.

The men viewed it both with and without a telescope, but could not discern whether it had a head or rippled back like that of an alligator. A former sea captain who had seen it along with the other men felt it could have been a grampus whale. Either way, it was impossible to say whether it was the same thing seen by Delano, who maintained that what he saw was definitely not a whale. Delano told a reporter from the *Charleston Mercury* he was familiar with all types of whales, but had only seen "a monster" similar to the one at St. Simons Island on one other occasion.[83] In this case he was at Doboy Sound, a body of water that separates Sapelo Island from the mainland and connects to the Altamaha River.

For nearly half a century following the Delano report, sightings were either rare or rarely reported, as there seems to be a significant quiet period. However, that would all change when a dramatic sighting made big headlines in 1981.

Rise of Altie

December in Georgia can be hit or miss when it comes to winter weather. Fortunately in December 1980, the temperatures were edging on 60 degrees Fahrenheit during the day. Larry Gwin and his friend, Steve Wilson, wanted to take advantage of this warm trend, so they headed out to Smith Lake, a tributary of the main river channel located about fifteen miles inland from the Atlantic coast, for some eel fishing.

As the men were fishing, they caught sight of something rising and swirling through the brackish water not far from their boat. It was not uncommon to see huge bass or even a sturgeon on the move, but this was not a normal fish, if a fish at all. It appeared to be snake-like with a brown-colored body about fifteen to twenty feet long. According to the men, it was "as big around as a man's body with two brownish humps about five feet apart."[84] The fishermen watched the odd creature for several moments until it finally dove in a "big swirl of water." As it descended, the water "boiled up a swell that was like a wake of a racing boat."

The sighting was so unusual that Gwin, who was a former newspaper publisher, made an official report to the press. The story was initially published in the local news, but was quickly picked up by the national press where it made quite a stir in early 1981. Could a creature like the Loch Ness Monster be hiding in the dark waters of the Altamaha? It would have seemed like a far-fetched proposition, if not for the string of credible witnesses who began to come forward with equally intriguing tales.

Two of these were Barry Prescott and Andy Green. About six months before Gwin and Wilson saw something, Prescott and Green were driving along Highway 95 near Darien when they caught sight of a very odd creature on the bank of Cathead Creek, a coastal tributary of the Altamaha. The creek was rather shallow at the time due to the low tide, and the thing appeared to be stranded on the muddy ground. The men watched as it thrashed and splashed, apparently trying to get itself back into the water.

The creature was so strange, they pulled off to get a better look. From their vantage point, they watched it periodically writhe around then lay still for several moments. They could clearly see it was dark in color with a skin that appeared to be rough or "warty."[85] It was approximately three to four feet thick and at least thirty feet long, based on what they could see extending out of the water, which was about twenty feet of the creature. They did not see any humps; only a triangle-looking section on the lower part of its body. They assumed "it had some sort of appendages, gills, or something below [the surface]" that enabled it to splash up a significant amount of water. "Its movement was powerful and undulating, rather than back and forth swimming movement of marine life," they recalled.

After about ten minutes the men were getting ready to depart when the thing finally freed itself from the bank and sank into the water without any further disturbance. They never saw it again.

Another witness who came forward was Harvey Blackman of Brunswick, Georgia. Blackman told syndicated columnist, Hugh Mulligan, he was fishing from a floating dock on the Altamaha, at a location called Two Way Fish Camp, when he was rocked by a sudden wave. The startled fisherman looked down to see a grayish-brown, "monstrous something," about fifteen to twenty feet long and as big around as a man in the water.[86] As it swam by, it raised its head above the surface for a moment. Its eerie visage looked like a "snake head."

Around the same time period in 1981, another witness reportedly saw a strange aquatic animal in another Altamaha creek just south of Two Way Fish Camp. The witness, who requested anonymity, told author and historian, Ann Davis, he and a friend were paddling along in a small boat when they saw something lying on the mud bank up ahead.[87] At first they thought it might be an alligator, but as they approached it became apparent it was not. This thing was about ten to twelve feet long and almost two feet in diameter with grayish-brown skin.

They immediately thought of the recent news reports concerning the alleged Altamaha-ha and thought perhaps they were seeing it for themselves. As they attempted to get closer, however, the animal slid back into the water and proceeded to swim right by their boat. The men could now see what appeared to be two or three humps on its body as it undulated along. They could not see any fins behind the head nor any appendages. It looked snake-like, but was definitely not a snake or an eel.

Once the creature was past the boat, it turned and "looked back," although it didn't raise its head up out of the water. The men were concerned it might return and attempt to hit the boat, but it simply turned and swam off down the channel.

Frank Culpepper, the owner of Two Way Fish Camp, cited another incident in which three men spotted a "big snake-looking creature" one day near the camp's dock.[88] Culpepper said he was inside a building when one of the men rushed in and told him to grab a rifle and get outside. Culpepper hurried outside with his rifle, but by then whatever it was had disappeared in the murky water.

"All I saw was the wake the creature left," Culpepper explained. "I have heard tales about seeing stuff on the river, and have thought about that incident at the camp a thousand times, but never got to see the monster, whatever it was."

Culpepper may have just missed it at the camp; however, he did experience a startling encounter with something while fishing upriver. He was sitting in his boat when something slapped the side with significant force. Culpepper looked down to see a thick, "long, brownish creature" moving in the water. It seemed as though it was trying to get into the boat.

"It scared me so badly, I cranked the boat and went back to the camp," Culpepper admitted. "It looked like a big snake."

Another spooky encounter was reported by Donny Manning. In an interview with Ann Davis, Manning said he and his brother were doing some night fishing from their father's houseboat in July of 1969 or 1970 when they hooked something big.[89] They were fishing for catfish at the time, using a special bait that consisted of oatmeal and soda pressed onto a three-pronged hook. When something took the bait and started pulling the line, they immediately noticed it was not the typical run-stop-turn motion of a catfish. In this case, the line just zipped forward with a great force.

Manning yanked the rod, causing the culprit to come up out of the water enough for the brothers to get a good look at it in the houseboat floodlights. What they saw was definitely not a catfish or even a sturgeon. The thing was approximately ten to twelve feet long with gray skin and a head like an alligator.

"It had a horizontal tail, instead of a fish-like vertical one, and had a spiny kind of bony triangular ridge along the top of its body, and a dorsal fin that was down on its back," Manning recalled. "The teeth were shining in the light and they were sharp pointed teeth. It was gun-metal gray on top and oyster white-yellow on bottom. It didn't move side to side like a snake, but up and down in a vertical motion—like a porpoise."

One might consider a misidentified alligator gar, but Manning was adamant the thing was not a gar. He had lived along the swampy waters of the Altamaha for most of his life and was familiar with just about every kind of aquatic life the area had to offer.

Manning momentarily fought with the creature as it yanked the line of his sturdy, saltwater rig, but he was no match. It eventually snapped the 40-lb test line and disappeared into the depths of the night.

Deepening Mystery

Whatever people were seeing along the Altamaha appeared to be extraordinary. The description of an extremely long, snake-like body, horizontal fins (or lack of fins), and a head that resembled an alligator but not an alligator did not match any particular type of marine animal indigenous to the Atlantic coast. It seemed like whatever it was hadn't previously been identified, whether it was an inhabitant of the Altamaha or something that had gained access via the sea.

The locals in and around Darien were excited by the news stories and open to the possibility a unique creature may be calling their seaport home, but experts were skeptical. They were quick to point out that sightings could be attributed to an unusually large sturgeon, a fish that did in fact populate the Altamaha. Others suggested a manatee. West Indian manatees migrated to the Altamaha estuary in the summer, so perhaps one had been exploring the feeder creeks. Others believed Altie may be a stray dugong, porpoise, seal, or an oversized eel. Some even suggested Altie was merely a conglomeration of river otters. Otters are known to swim in groups, and when doing so in a straight line it may appear to be a solid, contiguous form. Yet others leaned toward an alligator gar—a large fish that truly does look prehistoric.

If the eyewitness descriptions were accurate, it's hard to imagine a manatee, dugong, porpoise, seal, otter, or even an alligator would be confused with something that had a much more elongated, snake-like body. An extremely large eel might fit the bill, but it seems most people would recognize an eel, regardless of size. An alligator gar seemed to be the most reasonable culprit with its slender body and alligator-like mouth, yet many of the witnesses were fisherman who would have been familiar with this type of fish. The alligator gar, which can grow up to eight feet in length, also has noticeable scales and a pair of fins near its head; characteristics that were not given in the Altie descriptions.

The fact the Altamaha River could be accessed by the sea gave the phenomenon a credibility your average landlocked aquatic legend did not have. Even though a strange marine animal coming in from the ocean would not be indigenous to fresh water, it wasn't out of the question. Sharks have been known to travel a surprising distance up a river. Why couldn't something else? Perhaps it was a so-called "sea serpent," like those that had inspired many a sailor's tale, or a prehistoric relic that was not actually extinct. In 1938, fisherman off the coast of South Africa reeled in a bizarre-looking fish that turned out to be a coelacanth. The discovery shocked scientists, since the coelacanth was thought to have gone extinct at the end of the Cretaceous period over sixty-six million years ago!

As residents along the Altamaha debated the possibilities, historians suggested that perhaps sightings of a strange beast in the river were not exclusive to modern times. According to southern mystery authority, E. Randall Floyd, the Tama Indians of the area had a legend of a giant water monster described as "a giant snake which hissed and bellowed when frightened."[90] The Creek Indian tribes of the southeast believed water-dwelling snakes with exceptional strength lived in the rivers and creeks of the area.[91] Stories like these were told to early American explorers who recorded them in their travel journals. Though no one could say for sure, perhaps these stories had been based on sightings of something large and snake-like lurking in the very waters of the Altamaha.

No Laughing Matter

As the 1980s progressed, so did the growing case file for the Altamaha-ha. Not long after the first news stories broke, rumors circulated that a Boy Scout Troop had encountered a strange creature in the swampy tributaries back in the 1940s. Officials at the Reidsville State Prison were said to have seen an unidentified creature in the 1950s.[92]

Kathy Howard Strickland believed she saw Altie sometime around the late 1970s as she was driving across the Champney Bridge, which passes over inland portions of the Altamaha's winding path. As she looked toward the river, an unusual "fish" caught her eye. It was partially above the surface, just idling in the water. She said it was dark in color, like an eel, with a long neck, small head, and two distinct humps along the back. It was "prehistoric looking" yet "very natural looking in appearance" and not a man-made item or a fish simply floating in the water.[93] She estimated it was at least twenty feet in length and as big around as a person. It had no tail or fins that she could see.

Incidents picked up again when the *Darien News* reported a dramatic new sighting in 1983. A car salesman named Tim Sanders said he was driving across the same Champney Bridge on the afternoon of January 16 when he "spotted what he thought to be a porpoise playing near the river bank about 100 yards away."[94] Curious, Sanders pulled over to observe. As he watched, he realized it was not a porpoise but some kind of unusual creature. He was awestruck as it swam leisurely across the Altamaha River.

Sanders said it appeared to be about twenty to twenty-five feet in length and "about the size of the torso of a man." Its skin was dark in color and it had several humps about six to seven feet apart along its back. Sanders also noted what he thought was a "snout" at the tip of its head.

"The thing that threw me is I've never seen a fish that big," Tim told the reporter. He conceded it could have been a sturgeon, "but sturgeons never looked or swam like that."

In the summer of 1985, Isaac Bacon was fishing with his brother and sister in a tributary of the Altamaha known as Dence Creek when they noticed something laying on the muddy bank. It was low tide, so the bank was visible more than usual. The trio couldn't decide if it was a living creature, such as an alligator, or perhaps a partly submerged tire. Finally, it moved.

"It blew water out of its nostrils, which made bubbles," Bacon said in a report to Ann Davis. "Then it entered the water and went up-creek a ways and started scraping/eating fiddler crabs off the pier there."[95]

It eventually swam toward their boat, giving them a better look. According to Bacon, it was twelve to fourteen feet long and as "big around as a man's body" with skin the color of dark mud. They could see no gills, fins, or appendages. The creature was definitely snake-like, but had a head more like that of an alligator. Bacon's sister became frightened when the thing neared the boat, so they quickly left the area.

Darien News detailed a very credible report in their May 26, 1988 edition. Veteran crab fisherman Ralph DeWitt said on the afternoon of May 13 he had just checked his crab traps in Doboy Sound and was navigating his boat toward the mouth of the Carneghan River when he saw what appeared to be trash wrapped around a crab buoy. Curious, DeWitt steered toward it. When he got within about forty feet, he realized it was actually something alive. It suddenly "dipped into the water."[96]

The fisherman watched as the thing's blackish-brown body "arched up out of the water" and then dove back in, following its head like a serpent. It appeared to be at least twenty feet long. "With that, I backed off and asked myself did I see what I saw?" DeWitt said.

When the creature did not reemerge, DeWitt navigated into the river channel and started working traps. He was still spooked by the encounter, so all the while he kept looking back to the spot where he'd seen the creature. Finally, after about ten minutes, he saw the thing's head break the surface again. He dropped the traps and began motoring slowly in its direction. When he got within forty to fifty feet, "the eel shaped head, 'leisurely' dipped into the water followed by the roll of the sleek-looking body out of the water and diving into the depths of the Carneghan."

"It's like nothing I've ever seen before," affirmed DeWitt, who had been harvesting crabs in the area for more than fourteen years. "I've seen manatees, sturgeon, tarpon, turtles, porpoise and logs, but I have never seen anything like this."

DeWitt said it was similar to an eel, but considerably larger. He could only wonder what kind of beast may be lurking just under the surface as he resumed his work. "I kind of wish he hadn't shown himself to me," he admitted.

According to another report from the *Darien News*, a strange creature was seen again near the Champney River Bridge on December 18, 1992, at 10:45 a.m. Scotty Rogers told reporters he was driving across the bridge when he noticed a disturbance in the waters of the Altamaha below. At first he thought it might be a school of fish, but then "a big thing looking like a tractor-trailer inner tube standing on end started coming out of the water and looked like it came at least 8 feet out." When more of the creature emerged, it looked to be upwards of thirty feet in total length.

Rogers said the creature appeared to be a "brownish-gray in color" and had a very broad circumference. He could not see its head but had no doubt this was a unique animal, if in size alone. Like many of the witnesses, Rogers had years of fishing experience in the Altamaha area. "I have never seen anything like this before," he concluded.

And that seems to be the consensus. Whether it was an unknown creature or one that was extremely rare and unusual, it was something no one could identify. The phenomenon was not unique to the world, but one the locals could call their own.

Embracing the Legend

As sightings of the Altamaha-ha continued in the coming decades, it firmly established the creature as part the local culture, particularly in the small town of Darien where reports tended to cluster. Darien was established in 1736 and still retains a certain old-world, maritime charm with its picturesque landmarks, boat docks, and seafood restaurants. Along with the many waterways that converge there along the coast, it seems only natural that a mysterious "sea creature" would be part of the regional traditions.

The first cultural sign of the creature can be found at the Darien Visitor Center. A billboard displaying a huge rendition of the Altamaha-ha guides you into the parking lot of an outlet mall where the center is located. Inside the museum, you can find a fantastic museum-quality replica of Altie created by artist Rick Spears, an exhibit designer at the Fernbank Science Center. Spears based his design on witness descriptions, resulting in an impressive piece that Cindy and I were able to view in person during a trip to Darien.

The visitor center also provides a wealth of information on local attractions, including a nice trifold brochure on the subject of the Altamaha-ha. The brochure includes a rundown of the history and sightings, with a map to their locations. You can even buy a few Altie-related souvenirs.

The creature's similarity to the alleged Loch Ness Monster cannot go unnoticed, and perhaps there's a strange bit of irony here since the town was founded by Scottish Highlanders from the very shores of Loch Ness. According to official records, the original settlers were recruited at Inverness, Scotland, in 1735.[97] Inverness is situated at the mouth of the River Ness, which flows from legendary Loch Ness. The Highlanders even called their budding settlement New Inverness before changing its name to Darien!

As with Nessie, the Altamaha creature continues to stir up news reports. In March 2018, I got a call from *First Coast News* out of Jacksonville, Florida, asking me to comment on a photo of a strange carcass that had supposedly washed up on a beach in southeast Georgia. The photo, which had surfaced on the internet a day earlier, appeared to show the decaying body of an unknown marine animal that matched descriptions of the Altamaha-ha. According to WSB-TV Atlanta, which broke the story, a man named Jeff Warren spotted the deceased animal while boating with his son at Wolf Island National Wildlife Refuge in Golden Isles, Georgia. Warren said he first thought the creature was a dead seal, but upon closer inspection realized it was more of a "Loch Ness-type thing."[98]

With its long, snake-like body, small head, flippers, and tail fins, people were quick to surmise it may be a dead Altamaha-ha specimen. There was nothing in the photo to provide scale; however, at any size, it certainly resembles the collective image of Altie.

I told the news reporter I would be thrilled if it were an unknown species, but without speaking to the individual who supposedly discovered it, and better yet, examining the carcass myself, it's hard to say just what it is. It looked promising, but there was little I could glean from a single photo whose origin was unsubstantiated. Dan Ashe, director of the US Fish and Wildlife Service, conjectured it might be the remains of a basking shark that had decomposed "in a way where it looks like it has a long neck and tiny head, resembling a prehistoric creature." It wouldn't be the first time an oddly decomposed carcass was mistaken for a "sea serpent."

I tried to find out what happened to the supposed carcass, but I was never able to track it down. As in so many of these "mysterious photo" cases, it is often hard to determine if it is a real creature, a hoax, or merely an illusion created by the decaying body of a common animal.

During our visit to Darien a few years earlier, Cindy and I drove along US 17 where it's easy to find spots to pull over and view the Altamaha River. At each spot, we sat for a while gazing at the vast water and contemplating the possibility of Altie's reality. We had a video camera in hand, of course, just in case we spotted something.

We also traveled further up the river where we could access

a more remote spot on its wild banks. There we trudged through the reed grass and Ogeechee trees, marveling at the network of soggy channels covered in carpets of avocado-colored duck weed. Cindy noticed a small alligator moving through the one of the weedy offshoots. It watched us with two wary eyes peering above the surface of the water. Wildlife along the river was plentiful, and perhaps dangerous if one were to encounter something larger.

When we reached the bank, we found the remains of an old, weathered pier. We used it as a vantage point to survey the river, which spanned a good distance across and as far as we could see in either direction. The enormity of the Altamaha basin could only be imagined. This small section seemed vast enough, let alone the miles and miles of watery terrain that stretched further inland. It placed the phenomenon in perspective. Cindy and I both agreed: *anything* could be out there in the depths of the dark water.

Billboard advertisement in Darien, Georgia
(Photo by Lyle Blackburn)

Altamaha Hairy

Upriver from the sunny estuary at Darien and further back in the recesses of the Altamaha swamps, there seems to be a different type of mysterious creature lurking in the shadows; something covered in hair, yet walks upright like a man. The area is not necessarily *known* for Bigfoot, but according to witnesses, such a creature should also be included among the Altamaha legends.

Back in 1982, three friends were driving north of the river along Beards Creek Church Road in Tattnall County when they caught sight of something strange. It was around 11:00 p.m., and they were headed down an unpaved road toward the old cemetery behind Beards Creek Church. They'd heard some ghostly legends about the area, so they decided to drive out and investigate for fun. As they drove past the church building, they noticed the silhouette of someone or something standing in the glow of a nearby mercury lamp. It was upright and standing on two legs, but appeared to be larger than an average person. They immediately turned around to get a better look, curious as to who would be roaming around out there so late at night.

"As we headed toward this shadow, it took off running—still on two feet—toward the graveyard," recalled one of the witnesses.[99] They followed in the car, trying to get a better look. "We drove up next to a large headstone, and just as we thought we lost sight of this thing, it stood up from behind the headstone," the witness continued. "We froze as it stared at us."

Now they could see it was not a person. It was something that stood at least seven feet tall and had brown hair all over its body. Its eyes glowed red in the headlights as it stared intently at the teenagers.

"It only stood there for a few seconds and then turned and ran off into the woods," said the witness. "Needless to say after seeing it we did not try to follow."

The location is in the countryside of Glenville, Georgia, where the swampy tendrils of the Altamaha wind through the dark woods. It's a location that could easily obscure any wild beasts, including those that may currently be unknown.

In November 2008, approximately fifty miles downriver, Bill Burns and his uncle set out to deer hunt in the Sansavilla Wildlife Management Area of Wayne County. It was early evening around 5:00 p.m. as they trudged through the palmettos, eventually splitting up for separate locations. Burns's uncle headed off into the distance while Burns crossed two empty slough channels and sat down on the bank of the farthest one.

The evening air was unusually chilly and quiet as he began to scan the area. That's when he noticed a surprising figure standing a short distance away. It appeared to be a very tall man wearing a camouflage ghillie suit, although the suit looked more like hair than artificial foliage. As he looked on, he began to get the feeling it wasn't a human.

"He had hair all over and was standing beside a tree," the witness recalled.[100] "I made eye contact with him and I could see the left cheek of his face and he had a pointy nose and dark beady eyes."

A squirrel ran up behind Burns and made a noise, as if in distress. The hunter glanced briefly at the squirrel, and when he looked back to where the figure was standing, it was gone.

Burns sat there for a while, spooked by what he'd seen. He heard some splashing in the slough behind him but whatever was making the noise was obscured by a heavy thicket. He thought it might be a deer, but wasn't sure.

"It got dark on me before I realized it [and] said to myself 'get out of here,'" the hunter continued. "I stood up and walked toward the [splashing] and about 20 feet away in the thicket, in the darkness, this thing let out a growl that raised the hair on my arms. I can't explain the growl, but it was a growl of 'you are here and I am going to eat you.'" Needless to say, the hunter quickly fled from the area.

In an interview with longtime Bigfoot investigator Ken Johnson of Georgia, the witness described himself as an avid hunter who was familiar with the local wildlife. He was certain he was not hoaxed, since no one knew where he and his uncle were specifically going to hunt. He described the alleged creature as "as approximately seven feet tall, blackish in color, heavily built—'like a football player'—and covered with hair that appeared to be twelve to thirteen inches in length." It had dark, animal-like eyes with a "wild look" and grayish-colored skin on its face. If it were a man in a camouflage suit, he was convincing as a "Bigfoot" and not afraid of being shot. Burns could have easily hit him if he wanted to take a shot. However, he was just too frightened by the experience to think about firing.

When Burns told his uncle what he'd seen, his uncle confessed he'd seen something, too, which scared him so much he didn't really want to talk about it. Burns later spoke to a coon hunter who said others had also seen the creature, and they often referred to it as "Foots." If Burns was seeking comfort by sharing his story, it didn't help much. The conversations with others merely reinforced the notion that something big and unexplainable may be haunting the vast reaches of the Altamaha—both on land and in the water.

Cindy at the Altamaha River
(Photo by Lyle Blackburn)

7

BIG CYPRESS AND THE EVERGLADES

No swamp-themed book would be complete without including one of the most well-known of America's wild wetlands: the Everglades. Located in Florida, the Everglades and its associated habitats make up one of the largest wetland ecosystems in the country. This massive freshwater system, called the "River of Grass," is essentially a very shallow, slow-moving river approximately sixty miles wide and one hundred miles long.[101] It originates at Lake Okeechobee in central Florida and stretches all the way to the state's southern coast. Marsh prairies, cypress swamps, and mangroves can all be found within this amazing subtropical terrain.

As one would expect, the Greater Everglades ecosystem is home to a vast variety of animals and plants that thrive in its rich environment. The region's location at the confluence of temperate North America and the tropical Caribbean produces a diverse complex of flora, which includes nearly eight hundred types of native seed-bearing plants.[102] Bromeliads and epiphytic orchids are among the most colorful plants, while rockland forest pines are among the largest. Amid these are a number of grasses, sedges, ferns, shrubs, vines, and other trees that provide protection and sustenance for the resident creatures.

The first animal that comes to mind when thinking of the Everglades is undoubtedly the American alligator. This famous denizen is regarded as the keystone species and is perhaps the most iconic of all swamp dwellers.[103] The American crocodile can also be found here, along with the elusive Florida panther, whose numbers have unfortunately dwindled in recent years. Deer, hogs, foxes, tortoises, and many other wild species make up the rest of the population, along with a variety of indigenous—and a few invasive alien—snakes. Not to be overlooked, the Everglades is also known for its feathered population. As many as 347 bird species have been identified within its borders, including wood storks, ibises, herons, egrets, spoonbills, and bald eagles. It's truly a paradise of nature.

When I visited the Everglades at ten years old, I took an airboat ride with my father and grandfather. I can still recall my excitement as our boat captain zoomed us across the grassy waters. I remember marveling at the sheer expanse while trying to spot alligators in our wake. For a young boy, it was absolutely thrilling.

Alligator hunters in a mangrove swamp, 1882
(Courtesy of the State Library and Archives of Florida)

For the most part, the Everglades simply offers miles of marshland that bask in the light of the Florida sun. It's an attraction for tourists, thrill seekers, and naturalists. However, like any swamp, there are rumors of strange things that emanate from its darker corners. Stories of lost cities, ghosts, man-like apes, giant snakes, and alligator people date back to the very time when indigenous people first began to settle this vast, rich area. Even today these mysteries linger in the shrouded mangroves, making the Everglades one of the most intriguing destinations upon our swampy tour.

Lost and Found

In a swampland as big as the Everglades, it's not surprising some of its most tantalizing lore involves lost things and strange disappearances. Not only are there miles of it to get lost in, but in a land where so much of the ground is obscured by twisted roots, crowded reeds, and briny water, things can be easily concealed—or deceitfully hidden. From airplanes to human bodies, the Everglades has a long history of devouring that which comes its way.

Like Georgia's Okefenokee swamp, the Everglades is said to be a possible resting spot for the navy's ill-fated Lost Squadron, which disappeared during a routine training flight on December 5, 1945. According to two independent researchers, the five Avenger aircraft could have turned inland and flown in the direction of the Everglades after nightfall. If they ran out of gas above the swamp and crashed, the terrain could have easily swallowed them.

This theory seems as wild as any; however, the two aviation sleuths, Jon Myhre and Andy Marocco, have come across enough circumstantial evidence to suggest it might be plausible. Marocco used navy documents to determine "the USS Solomons aircraft carrier, while off the coast of Daytona Beach, picked up a radar signal from four to six unidentified planes over North Florida, about 20 miles northwest of Flagler Beach."[104] Based on information that indicates the planes turned to a compass heading of 170 degrees (southeast) while flying at 135 mph, the two men calculated at least one of the planes could have crashed within miles of where an unidentified Grumman Avenger torpedo bomber was actually found in 1989.[105] The surprising wreckage was spotted by a Broward County sheriff's helicopter pilot as he flew over the Everglades near the Alligator Alley toll road. When the downed plane was inspected at the time, no tail number or engine serial numbers could be found, so there was no way to determine if it was one of the Lost Squadron.

Myhre and Marocco still feel it is a possibility based on their examination of photos that were taken of the wreck. One of the photos shows the cockpit, which is undoubtedly that of a TBM-3 Avenger, the exact model flown by Lt. Charles Taylor, the commander of Flight 19. The only problem now is locating the wreck to corroborate this information. Since its discovery in 1989, the downed plane has gone missing—either swallowed up by the swamp or pillaged by souvenir hunters who converged on the area after the discovery was made public. If it can be found and reexamined, perhaps the Everglades can claim itself as the final resting place for the most enigmatic of aviation mysteries.

In addition to lost planes, the Everglades also boasts a lost city hidden within the overgrown reaches of Broward County. Located near Alligator Alley, the lost city—also known as "Ghost Village"—was once a large Seminole village that was inexplicably abandoned. Objects found there date back thousands of years, indicating it was once a thriving settlement. Yet there's no explanation as to why the inhabitants left, presumably during the height of its prosperity.

In the years since, the site has been used for various nefarious purposes such as hiding stolen gold and manufacturing bootleg alcohol. According to Ron Bergeron, former head of the Florida Fish and Wildlife Conservation Commission, during the Civil War a group of Confederate soldiers hid out there after stealing gold from the Union.[106] The location was certainly good for concealment but turned out to be a very bad choice. According to legend, the Seminoles suddenly materialized from the swamp and killed the entire party in a gruesome massacre. They considered the land sacred ground and would tolerate no invaders. The whereabouts of the gold, if any, remains a mystery.

In the early 1900s, a band of criminals claimed the location as a secret base for making illegal alcohol. Some believe the operation was masterminded by the notorious Chicago gangster, Al Capone, who owned a drinking and dancing establishment on Loop Road off the Tamiami Trail during the Prohibition era. The lost city is positioned on high ground within the protective swamp, so it would have been ideal to manufacture booze there and transport it by wagon to his saloon. All that remains of the moonshining operation today are some abandoned shacks and old distilling equipment.

Criminal activity in the region extends well beyond moonshining, however, into more macabre realms. The most chilling of these cases involved a man by the name of Edgar Watson. Watson, who was originally from South Carolina, came to the Everglades in the 1880s and built a cabin on the remote island of Chokoloskee along the alligator-infested banks of the Chatham River. The island was peppered with numerous Native American burial mounds, and Watson had no qualms about constructing his swampy home atop one of these sacred sites.

In the years to follow, the handsome-yet-eccentric Watson mostly kept to himself, making a living raising pigs, hunting alligators, and growing sugar cane. A small community was located nearby, mostly formed by the most undesirable dredges of society who relocated here for the island's relative obscurity and promised anonymity. Watson would occasionally venture to the town to sell his goods, but even in this dubious settlement he was regarded with suspicion and distrust. There was something about

Watson that just didn't sit right with those who encountered him. Stories that he'd killed several people before retreating to the Everglades circulated. Among the rumored victims was Belle Starr, the famous female gunslinger widely known as "The Queen of the Outlaws." Watson supposedly gunned her down in Arkansas, and others he supposedly killed with his bare hands during bar brawls.

Watson's sugar business began to thrive when he started bottling the cane syrup. The demand allowed him to expand his plantation and hire workers to help with the harvest and bottling operations. After a few seasons, the locals began to notice a peculiar pattern in which the labor force would inexplicably disappear at the end of the harvest season, or in some cases, even before. This bolstered speculation that rather than pay them, Watson would kill them and throw their bodies into the murky swamp, or worse, feed them to the alligators. It became known among the morbid as the "Watson Payday."

When a human skeleton was eventually found floating in the swamp near Watson's home, the locals questioned him. Watson suggested it was probably one of the many Native American remains that were scattered about the area. Without any way to confirm the identity or to even determine the age of the bones, neither the townsfolk nor the law could do much about it.

Gruesome discoveries began to add up, however. A short time later, some squatters who had been camping on Watson's property were found shot to death. Once again, Watson was confronted but denied having anything to do with it.

Suspicions finally transformed to action in 1910 when a fisherman found the corpse of a woman rotting in the fetid waters of the swamp. She had apparently been murdered, cut open and gutted. The woman, identified as Hannah Smith, had definitely worked for Watson. When another of his workers, an ex-con named Dutchy Melvin, was found dead, the heat intensified. At that point, one of Watson's employees came forward claiming he'd actually seen the shady sugar mogul kill someone. He said Watson gutted the victim so the body would sink in the dark waters. The worker insisted the swamp was virtually littered with the corpses of Watson's unfortunate and unpaid victims.

Fed up with a lack of police action, the townsfolk organized a posse of twenty men who intended to apprehend Watson and deliver him to the local sheriff so he could face justice. When they converged on his home, armed and nervous, Watson protested his innocence as usual, but this time he supposedly raised a shotgun and attempted to fire it. The weapon misfired, but that did not stop the posse from filling him full of lead, killing him instantly. As the story goes, they tied his corpse to the back of a boat and dragged him to a place called Little Rabbit Key where they buried him in a muddy pit.

After the Watson lynching the murders ceased, but to this day no one can be sure whether Watson was indeed the perpetrator or it was someone else. In totaling up the body count—which is said to include a few runaways, two game wardens, a "crazy" Frenchman, a man named Green Waller, Hannah Smith, and poor Dutchy Melville—it comes to a total of fifty-three.[107] If this is accurate and true, it would make Watson the second-most-prolific serial killer in United States history behind Gary Ridgway, the "Green River Killer."

Over the years, Watson's story has grown into modern murder lore, spawning a trilogy of books by Peter Matthiessen and a small tourist industry around the area of the Chokoloskee, where a modest museum offers information and tours of Watson's old stomping grounds. Whether Watson really committed the murders or not, his presence left a bloody stain on the Everglades. And perhaps he's never left. His old plantation is said to be haunted not only by Watson himself, but the spirits of his victims who were tossed into the black waters of the unforgiving bog, never to be found.

Gruesome as it is, Watson's alleged victims aren't the only bodies to surface in the shadows of the Everglades. Throughout the years, numerous bones and bodies have turned up, many of them showing signs of grisly murder. For example, in the span of just six months in 1977, four bodies were discovered near Alligator Alley. On July 25, a group of Native Americans was hiking through the woods between Alligator Alley and US 41 when they came upon the corpse of a man.[108] They were shocked to find two bullet holes in his head. The next day, a skeleton wearing a gold chain was found in the nearby brush. The cause of death in this case was never determined. In November and December, two female skeletons were found. Authorities felt they might have a serial killer on the loose, but there was no way to connect the bodies, especially since they were unidentified.

Disappearances seem commonplace as well, with a good number of locals and tourists having gone missing in the Everglades over the years. This may seem natural considering the formidable terrain and slithering dangers, but most of these disappearances cannot be attributed to people hiking too far into the vast reaches where even the most rugged individuals would have a hard time. Disappearances can occur even at the edges.

Take, for example, the case of 67-year-old Roger Sawyer. On March 5, 2011, Roger was camping with his family at the Everglades National Park in Flamingo when he inexplicably vanished.[109] Sawyer was a retired butcher from Oregon who had been traveling through Florida in a motor home with his wife, son, and daughter-in-law. While at the park, some of the family members went to the Visitors Center while Roger and his wife, Paula, stayed behind. Roger and Paula eventually ended up in different areas of the park, but no one thought much of it until it started getting dark and everyone returned to the motor home except Roger.

The family began to look for him immediately, but no trace of Roger could be found. He was an experienced outdoorsman and in good health and of sound mind, so it was odd he would have wandered off or gotten lost that easily. After searching for him themselves, the family sought help from park officials who summoned the Miami-Dade Fire Rescue department.

The US Park Service led the initial search, which lasted the rest of the evening and into the next day. They combed the beach area at the south end of the park where it terminates into the Florida Bay and canvased the mangroves that surround it to the north. But there was no sign of Roger. A more extensive search was launched thereafter, lasting nearly 10 days before authorities finally gave up. Roger was simply gone, either having been swallowed up by the cruel twists of the mangroves or perhaps abducted, though no one really believed that was the case.

Just five months later another man went missing. It started on August 30, 2011, when authorities found an abandoned pickup truck near Evergreen Lake in the Everglades National Park.[110] After determining the truck belonged to Tracy Olivier—a young man from Spring, Texas—they mounted an extensive search of the area to try and locate him. Authorities used triangulation technology from Olivier's cell phone to narrow the search within eleven and a half miles of the vehicle. Forty-five people, along with helicopters and tracking dogs, combed the mangrove mazes looking for the missing teen but came up empty-handed. To date, both Tracy Olivier and Roger Sawyer are still missing.

Ghostly Visions and Voices

As much as dead bodies are associated with the backwaters of the Everglades, so are ghosts. We've already learned of the ghostly rumors floating around Bloody Watson and his alleged victims, but there are plenty more to go around. Perhaps the most fantastic is the tale of a ghostly pirate ship said to navigate the twisted channels of the Everglades as punishment for the crew's horrible crimes. The legend originated in the 1800s and was told by sailors who navigated the bays and river channels of the Florida coast. According to the story, a band of cutthroat pirates was sailing in the area when they came upon a merchant ship. They began to chase the ship, but it proved to be difficult to catch. Finally, after hours of pursuit, the pirates caught up to the vessel and boarded it. The pirate captain was so furious, he forced the merchant crew to walk the plank one by one while the skipper's wife watched. Horrified, the skipper's wife pleaded to God asking him to curse the pirates and damn them for eternity. When the pirates had completed their evil work and returned to their ship, a huge wave suddenly rose up and forced their craft into the labyrinthine swamp channels of the coastal Everglades. The pirates became trapped and eventually perished, but their souls and their ship were doomed to remain in the clutches of the 'Glades. Since then, people have reported seeing the hazy form of ghostly ship as it navigates the endless channels of mangrove and saw grass.

The reality of the ghost ship legend may be questionable, but the fate of Eastern Airlines Flight 401 is definitely not. On December 29, 1972, the Tristar jet was flying over the Everglades when the flight crew became aware of a malfunction in the landing-gear system. While they were troubleshooting the problem, no one noticed the autopilot mechanism had been turned off. The plane had already lost considerable altitude and by the time anyone noticed they were flying dangerously low, it was too late. The jet slammed into the marsh at 227 miles per hour, killing ninety-seven passengers along with two flight attendants and the first officer. Pilot Robert Loft and Flight Engineer Donald Repo initially survived, however, Loft died as he was pulled from the wreckage and Repo died later after succumbing to critical injuries.[111]

Since then, witnesses have reported seeing ghostly figures not only in the area where the plane went down but aboard aircraft that utilized salvaged parts from Flight 401 for maintenance. In these cases, descriptions of the eerie entities seemed to match either Pilot Robert Loft or Flight Engineer Donald Repo. In one chilling incident, a female passenger noticed a man in a flight uniform sitting in a nearby row who looked pale and ill. She alerted a flight attendant, who promptly came to check on him. When the attendant arrived, the mysterious man faded from view as the woman, the flight attendant, and several other passengers watched. The female passenger became so hysterical she had to be restrained. When she finally calmed down she was shown photos of various airline staff members to see if she could possibly identify him. She pointed to a photo of Donald Repo and told the attendant, "That's him."

In another instance, the ghost of Donald Repo seemingly warned of an impending problem aboard an Eastern L-1011 Tristar jet. He appeared this time inside the galley oven while a flight attendant was preparing meals. Terrified, she alerted several of the flight crew who also saw the apparition when they came to her aid. One of these was the flight engineer, who had actually known Repo in life. He immediately recognized the ghostly apparition as that of his former coworker. As the crew members watched in shock, Repo's ghost allegedly uttered the phrase: "Watch out for fire on this airplane."[112] Later, one of the plane's engines actually caught fire and the plane was forced to land prematurely. Repo's otherworldly prediction had indeed come true.

Creepy occurrences have also been reported at the spot where Flight 401 went down. Workers and passersby claim to have heard crying and moaning sounds emanating from the swamp, and occasionally blood-chilling screams.[113] They've also noted unexplainable drops in temperature and spotted strange orbs of light and ghostly figures moving through the reeds. The spirits of Flight 401, it seems, will never truly rest in their soggy grave.

Elsewhere in the Everglades, a solitary spirit is said to haunt its winding canoe trails. The entity, which has become known as the Everglades Ghost Boy, was allegedly seen by a young man in 2008 while he and his family were canoeing one afternoon. According to the witness, his family had come to the Everglades National Park earlier that morning and rented two canoes. He was in a canoe with his aunt and cousin, while his father, mother, and sister were in the other. As they were paddling the calm waters, the boy noticed something moving below the surface. When he looked down, he saw "a human figure" swimming alongside the canoe.[114]

"The water was extremely shallow [and] the figure moved like it had all the room in the world," the witness reported. "[It was] stretching 'its' arms out wide, legs extended, and 'it' was doing that even though there were walls of sand and mangrove trees everywhere."

The eerie swimmer appeared to be a young boy about thirteen years old with "beautiful blonde hair." The witness gasped as he watched it move next to the canoe. Suddenly, the swimmer looked up. He had dark red eyes with black circles around them.

"I sensed evil, and sadness, and very much cruelty," the witness said. "On seeing me, the boy turned his head and swam away, deeper into the water, fading away."

Once the swimmer was gone, the young man noticed his family was looking at him with concern. Apparently he had a look of shock on his face. His mother called from the canoe next him and asked if he was okay. He said he'd seen something in the water that scared him, but it was gone now.

The family dismissed the incident and continued on paddling and enjoying the scenery. However, within five minutes the witness caught sight of the ghostly boy again, this time peering at them from the thick trees that lined the canoe trail. The figure was staring intently with bright-red eyes and an angry face.

Before the witness could react or say anything to his family, the wind suddenly picked up out of nowhere and blew hard with a noticeable chill. It was so forceful, the canoes began to rock in the water. His cousin, who was standing up in the boat filming the scenery, lost her balance and fell overboard. The family shouted and the witness leaned over and yelled for his cousin to take his hand. She regained her composure, swam back to the canoe, and grabbed his hand. Once she was safely back in the boat the witness looked back at the trees, but the ghost boy was nowhere to be seen.

The rest of the day's canoeing was far less eventful, although the witness kept a wary eye on the waters and woods, fearing the ghostly entity might return. When they arrived back at the canoe rental place, the witness's cousin began to complain of an aching back. When her mother looked under her shirt, she was surprised to find that her back was purple and bruised. It looked as though she'd been hit or had run into something, but she could not recall any such injury. The boy thought back to the angry-looking ghost, feeling somehow it must have been responsible. He decided to keep quiet, however, and said nothing to his family.

A few years later, the witness returned to the boat rental place, and while he was there, he told one of the workers about his strange sighting. The worker didn't seem all that surprised. He said several years ago a boy was playing with his friends near the spot where they had been canoeing. When his friends placed a bet to see who could go under water and hold their breath the longest, the young boy tried to win, but ended up drowning. He was from a poor family, and winning a bet for money was something he desperately wanted. Perhaps it was a tragedy that left him swimming the mangrove-choked waters forever more.

A park ranger on airboat patrol in the Everglades, 1953 (Courtesy of the State Library and Archives of Florida)

Planet of the Skunk Apes

In 1957, a group of hunters ventured into the Big Cypress Swamp Preserve on the west side of the Everglades. It was a rugged and remote place, but one that promised excellent game for any hunters brave enough to endure its challenge. After the day's hunt, the men set up camp and built a fire. Later they suspended their hammocks between the cypress trees and set in for a night of well-earned rest. It would hardly be restful, however.

During the night, the men "were awakened by heavy footfalls and splashing and breaking branches."[115] Alarmed, they quickly got out of their hammocks, grabbed their firearms, and crouched with their backs to the fire. As the footsteps approached, the hunters could see a dark silhouette in the shape of a large man between the trees about thirty feet away. Their first thought was that it was a Seminole Indian, but upon studying it, they felt it was too big to be a human. It was man-like, yet bulkier and apish.

The thing lingered among the cypress for approximately two minutes before it turned and walked away. As it did, the hunters could see its "head had a different shape, sort of a slump with what also seemed like a heavy chin." They weren't sure what it was, but they were sure it was something they'd never seen before—perhaps something that lived only in the remotest parts of the sprawling Everglades.

Unbeknownst to the hunters at the time, tales of an ape-like creature said to inhabit the forests and swamplands of Florida had long been circulating around the state. Generally described as being large, covered in hair, and looking like a cross between a man and an ape, the creature was said to have a foul odor and a reclusive nature which kept it in the shadows just beyond proof.

Stories such as these can be traced all the way back to the original, native inhabitants. According to *Explore Southern History* online, early Florida Indians told settlers of "a strange man-like creature that roamed remote swamps and woods. Covered with hair and much taller than normal humans, the monster was considered dangerous, and most who encountered him would not approach him."[116] Later, as the European settlers began to displace the tribal natives, newspapers documented accounts of strange ape-like creatures. In 1818 an "unknown animal" was discovered around Apalachicola, Florida. The animal managed to escape, but those who saw it said it resembled a "baboon."[117]

These elusive southern creatures would eventually become known as "Skunk Apes." The precise origin of the term *Skunk Ape* has been debated among paranormal scholars, but it's certain the term dates back to at least 1971 when the newspapers began using the name to describe a presumed population of these animals that were being reported more and more frequently in the Sunshine

State.

Not surprisingly, some of the most intriguing Skunk Ape sightings have come from the Everglades swamps. In the very same area along the Big Cypress Preserve, five members of the Peninsular Archaeological Society were camping on a cool night in February 1971 when they, too, saw something strange. They'd spent the day searching for Native American relics and were now sleeping peacefully in two tents. At around 2:30 a.m. one of the men in the smaller tent was awakened by movement outside. It sounded like someone—or some*thing*—walking around on the mound they'd been excavating. He decided to get up and take a look.

According to the group's president, H.C. "Buz" Osbon: "He looked out the tent flap and saw what appeared to be a big man, standing about eight feet away in the moonlight."[118] It struck him as odd, both the appearance of the "man" and fact that he was walking around outside so late. Assuming it had to be one of the men from the other tent, the archaeologist got back into his sleeping bag and closed his eyes. Moments later, he heard "what sounded like a number of people all talking at once." The voices were strange and alarming.

The man bolted upright and woke up his tent-mate. They both looked outside, but whatever had been there before was gone. The men rushed to wake the guys in the second tent and told them what had happened. "We looked around but saw nothing," Osbon continued.

The next morning the men found a set of strange tracks where the figure had been lurking. They were very "man-like" but also very huge, measuring seventeen and a half inches long and eleven inches wide. The men retrieved some plaster and made casts of the footprints.

Osbon told reporters that he and his associates had "heard rumors about some kind of apeman running loose in the swamp" for years.[119] He never paid much attention to the rumors until the incident at the mound. He was now convinced they'd had an encounter with one of these legendary beasts. On a subsequent trip to the Big Cypress Swamp, members of the Archaeological Society found two sets of smaller tracks. Osbon speculated there were at least three of these ape-like creatures in the area.

Not long after Osbon's group reported their incident, authorities responded to a call from residents living sixteen miles west of Fort Lauderdale on the eastern border of the Everglades. According to news reports, a boy and girl allegedly spotted two ape-like creatures near their home at King's Manor Estate Trailer Court along the North New River Canal. The animals were described as having "monkey's faces, long arms, small eyes, gray splotches all over, and being 'taller than daddy,' or more than six feet tall."[120] Local residents quickly formed a posse to track down the creatures but had no luck.

In response to the hubbub, the Florida Highway Patrol asked Henry Ring, a county animal control officer, to conduct a search for the animals. During his investigation, Ring reportedly found "a bunch of strange tracks, like someone was walking around on his knuckles."[121] Later, in August 1971 while driving ten miles west of Fort Lauderdale, Ring apparently had a firsthand sighting. "I saw this thing around midnight," he told a reporter from the *National News*.[122] "It walked like an ape, with long arms dangling nearly to the ground—but somehow stood straighter than an ape."

According to Bob Carr, a former Miami-Dade County official archaeologist and area historian, residents in the Davie area (on the east side of the Everglades) should be on alert. "I talked to one gentleman who was a security guard [in the early 1970s], working at a trailer park next to an orange grove," Carr told a reporter from the *Miami News* in 1998. "He saw a large gorilla-type creature pulling a dead cow into a ditch at night while he was doing a patrol in his car."[123]

The incidents would only get stranger. At 3:30 a.m. on January 9, 1974, the Florida Highway Patrol received a call from a motorist who said he saw a tall, hairy creature limping along US Route 27 near the Dade-Broward County border in the eastern portion of the Everglades. According to a *Miami News* article, the call came from a truck stop where troopers and sheriff's deputies converged a short time later.[124]

As the authorities were checking out the first claim, a second call came in from thirty-five-year-old Richard Lee Smith, who claimed he had "struck a two-legged creature" with his Cadillac on the same road. Troopers were skeptical of Smith's claim since his car only had "a kind of brush mark" on one fender, but the calls were enough to warrant a search using personnel on the ground and two helicopters with powerful searchlights. During the search, Hialeah Gardens Patrolman Robert Holmeyer said he had personally arrived at the scene while it was still dark and saw a "shadowy, dark, 8-foot tall creature thrashing off into the underbrush." Holmeyer said he wasn't sure what it was, but "it made a lot of noise thrashing about," and he didn't feel he should go in after it in the dark.[125]

Around the same time as the police hunt in Dade County, dozens of huge footprints were discovered at a catfish farm near the Everglades National Park. The prints, which measured "twelve inches long and seven and a half inches across, with a stride length of five feet," were examined by several experts, all of whom could not explain what kind of animal had left them.

"It's beyond my comprehension that something could make a footprint that big," Everglades National Park Superintendent Jack Stark told the South Dade *News-Leader*. "I personally tend to disbelieve in the Skunk Ape or yeti, [but] I wouldn't say it's not the Skunk Ape—the discovery remains an unsolved mystery of the Everglades."[126]

A few months later, on March 24, 1975, Ronald Bennett,

his son Michael, and their friend Lawrence Groom were driving down a dirt road toward Black Point around midnight when "they observed what appeared to be a giant ape-like man approximately eight (8) to nine (9) feet tall and very heavy set, black in color with no clothes standing next to a blue Chevy and rocking the car back and forth with great force."[127]

As they approached, a man got out of the Chevy and started yelling hysterically for help. Seconds later, the ape-like man turned and ran into the mangrove trees. The witnesses continued down the road and eventually turned around. When they passed the Chevy again, they could hear movement in the mangroves but could no longer see the owner of the Chevy. Ronald Bennett eventually called police at 2:26 a.m., at which time a patrol officer was dispatched to the location. He searched the area but found no trace of the Chevy—or the ape-man. This bizarre report is still on file with the Dade County Public Safety Department.

In the years since the Skunk Ape first captured media attention, reports of these mysterious anthropoids have continued to seep from the swampy marshes of the Everglades, as well as many other areas of Florida. In a case investigated by my colleague, David Bakara, several men had a long and rather spooky encounter with one of these alleged creatures in 1995. It was spring of that year when Robert Kurly (RK) and a few friends took a trip to the Flamingo campground located within Everglades National Park. After camping, boating, and hiking the men decided to take a short nap near the camp's entrance before driving back to their home in Miami.

"About an hour into my nap I was awakened by my friend who appeared panicked and was motioning me not to make a sound," RK said. "He was shaking and pointing at the glass where my head was touching the window."[128]

RK slowly turned his head to see an ape-like creature trying to peer into the driver's side window just inches from where his head had been moments before. The window of his sports car was heavily tinted, so it was possible to see out, but the creature could not see in.

RK and the other passengers were shocked and horrified by what they saw. The creature had a huge face with a large, broad nose and hair covering everything but the eyes and cheeks. It was breathing heavily, and the moisture from its breath fogged the outside of the glass.

"The ape-like creature was touching the car and continued to try to see in for a good five to ten minutes," RK continued. The frightened men simply watched in disbelief, trying to figure out just what it was. It looked somewhat like a gorilla, but was definitely not a gorilla or any other ape they'd ever seen.

The creature finally moved away from the car and walked to a dumpster about fifteen feet away where it began rummaging through the garbage. At this point they got a look at its whole body. RK explained that: "It had very long arms and was over six feet tall covered in a reddish-brown blondish fur [that was] shaggy looking."

The men watched as the ape-like thing continued to sift through the garbage, apparently looking for food. It occasionally paused to nibble on something before resuming its digging. At one point, it picked up a McDonalds bag and ripped it apart before throwing it on the ground. After a while, the thing gave up and headed off into the swampy prairie that surrounded the parking area.

RK wished he could have taken a photo, but his cell phone at the time did not include a camera. The only camera they had was in the trunk of the car with the rest of their luggage, and nobody wanted to move or get out while the creature was present.

While RK had not been able to take a photo, others would. On the morning of July 21, 1997, Ochopee Fire District Chief Vince Doerr was driving to work through the Big Cypress

Swamp Preserve when a "tall, hairy, reddish-brown thing" crossed the road in front of him.[129]

"It came from the left, which is the east, and then went across the road," Doerr told *Miami News* reporter Jim Kelly. "When it crossed the road, it looked like it was taking kind of long steps."

It didn't appear to be a bear, so Doerr stopped his truck and grabbed the camera sitting beside him in the cab. He always carried it in case he had to document a fire or an accident scene. He jumped out and looked through the viewfinder. The animal was approximately four hundred feet away.

"It kind of stopped, turned a little bit, and then it started north, parallel to the road," Doerr explained. "I had to turn my light meter on, then I adjusted and I snapped one picture. I looked at [the creature again], and it was kind of a small brown spot."

Knowing it would be pointless to take more shots, Doerr got back in his truck and continued driving. He wasn't convinced he'd seen a so-called Skunk Ape but did discuss the incident with several coworkers who must have told others. When the word got out, Doerr received a call from a reporter with the local *Everglades Echo* newspaper. After he told her what he'd seen, the reporter told him about two other incidents. First, Jan Brock, one of Doerr's neighbors, said she saw the same sort of creature on the same road several minutes before the fire chief estimated his sighting had taken place. According to Brock, who worked as a county realtor, she was driving to work at 7:45 a.m. when an upright creature crossed approximately one thousand feet in front of her car.[130] She said it was about seven feet tall and covered in thick, dark brown hair with what appeared to be a lighter colored patch on its chest. She had often seen wildlife in the area and was sure this was not a bear, noting that its legs were too long, and it walked for a long distance as it crossed the road and headed for the trees.

Less than two hours later, twenty tourists in a van driven

by Naples Trolley Tour guide John Vickers spotted it two miles away. As they were driving parallel to the Turner River Canal, they saw the thing run from east to west across Turner River Road. A short time later, Vickers was escorting most of the passengers on a "gator walk" along the canal when the creature emerged from some bushes about thirty yards from the parked van and frightened three people—two woman and a young girl—who had stayed behind. Vickers ran back to the van when the girl began screaming but was too late to see the thing himself. He could, however, see the fear and panic on the little girl's face, so he cut the tour short and drove to the local ranger station to report what they had seen.

The area where Doerr and the others had their encounter is a short distance from where longtime Skunk Ape hunter Dave Shealy said he and his brother first saw one of the elusive creatures in 1973. Only ten years old at the time, Shealy was hunting with his brother when they spotted a tall, upright subject entering the Turner River Swamp.

Shealy, whose family roots in the Everglades date back to 1891, has since dedicated much of his life to the pursuit and research of the Skunk Ape, which he claims to have laid eyes on two more times. Nowadays Shealy is head of the Trail Lake Campground located in Ochopee where he operates a small museum and gift shop known as the Skunk Ape Headquarters. Here visitors can book a guided tour of the surrounding marshlands and view an array of alleged evidence, including footprint casts. He has yet to find conclusive proof, but he's still active in the pursuit, along with others.

In August 1997, James McMullen said he was tracking panthers in the Everglades when "he came across a nearly 7-foot, 500-pound hairy creature" resembling a Bigfoot.[131] McMullen, a fifty-five-year-old naturalist and author of a book on Florida's panthers, was sloshing through a remote area located south of Lake Okeechobee and north of Ten Thousand Islands when he was surprised by the creature. The thing lingered for approximately thirty seconds before it slipped back into the recesses of the swamp.

McMullen told reporters he was unable to snap a photo of it, but has since found footprint evidence that suggests the beast is something related to Bigfoot. He made a plaster cast of the track, which has five toes and measures fourteen inches long. McMullen said he'd seen quite a few unexplainable things throughout the years while tracking panthers, but until the Skunk Ape sighting, he'd never come forward with any reports. The sighting and footprint was enough to convince him that a creature does exist and it may be in danger of extinction due to "overdevelopment and destruction of habitats that exist in critical areas of Florida."

The question of existence may be scientifically debatable, but there's no doubt Skunk Apes are an integral part of the Everglades' mystique as sightings continue to be reported. On the evening of November 11, 2010, a driver traveling along the outskirts of the Everglades saw a hairy bipedal figure cross the road in three huge strides.[132] It was after dark—around 10:30 p.m.—but the thing was visible in the headlights as it came out of the swamp on one side of the road and ran into a thicket on the other. It never looked in the direction of the car. The man sped away, wondering just what kind of animal he'd seen.

In November 2012, Albert Collins was target shooting in the Everglades west of Broward County when he caught sight of a "man-like ape standing behind a tree looking at him."[133] It stood upright on two legs and appeared to be approximately six-and-a-half feet tall with dark brown hair covering its body. Its face was an eerie cross between ape and man. It was enough to send Collins running for his car.

"As I got to my car, I saw the thing running behind the trees away from me and then I left in a hurry," Collins told my colleague David Bakara in a personal interview. It was something Collins would never forget.

The Big Cypress area of the Everglades still seems to be a focal point for these encounters, and perhaps that makes the most sense. The area has swaths of solid ground with huge pines, mingled with miles of swampy waters and shadowy corners where just about anything could hide—if it wanted to.

One evening in December 2014, a hunter and his nephew were walking out of Big Cypress when they saw something they would never forget. They were cutting through the woods toward Tamiami Trail when they came to a clearing. At that point the hunter's nephew decided to run ahead so he could take a look at the other end of the field before they continued to the trail. As he did so, the hunter happened to look back at the area where they'd just come. When he did, he was startled to see a large, upright figure.

"I noticed a movement from the distance," the hunter reported. "It was walking big steps right where we had hiked."[134]

The figure was large, bulky, and had arms that hung down to its knees. It walked upright, yet looked like an ape. The hunter became frightened and immediately called to his nephew, urging him to come back quickly as the sun was starting to go down. He never took his eyes off the thing. It just stood lingering in the trees. The hunter considered taking a shot at it, but decided it was too risky. What if it was a man in some kind of costume or ghillie suit? He didn't want to take a chance.

When his nephew returned, the hunter pointed out the figure that was still standing there, watching. The nephew took one look, then they both starting running. By the time they reached the trail, nightfall had effectively engulfed the area. To their relief, a man came by on a four-wheeler and stopped to give them a ride to their car. After conversing, the man invited them to eat dinner with some friends at his nearby hunting club. The hunters agreed.

Later during dinner, the witness worked up the courage to ask if anyone else had seen something resembling an ape in the Big

Cypress. Their host simply grinned and warned the hunter and his nephew to never go out there alone at night. Are there man-like apes lurking in the depths of the Everglade swamps? To this day no one can say for sure.

Artist interpretation of a Skunk Ape
(Illustration by D.W. Frydendall)

Scales and Slithers

Ape-men and alligators aside, one of the most iconic swamp dwellers is surely the snake. Along with their ubiquitous physical presence, these serpents have come to symbolize the inevitable dangers inherent in these primitive landscapes. Whether it's a piece of artwork or a movie featuring a swamp setting, snakes are almost always included.

Swamps typically contain a variety of snakes, and the Everglades is no different. The region has twenty-three indigenous species in all, with four of them being venomous: the Florida cottonmouth, the coral snake, the dusky pigmy rattlesnake, and the eastern diamondback rattler. Each one of these snakes is important because they help maintain the balance of nature and aid in the control of rodents and invertebrates. They also provide a food source for other animals such as alligators and birds.

Even though the presence of snakes in swamps is clearly beneficial to the ecosystem, they do add a definite risk. One must be especially cautious when walking through the boggy bottoms to avoid encounters with the venomous varieties. Most times an encounter is harmless, but there are times when a startled animal will react with its instincts. This is understandable, though, when one is accustomed to the natural order of these wild and ageless places.

There is, however, one slithery threat in the Everglades that should not be there. A monstrous, nonindigenous snake who has invaded the natural order—the Burmese python. These foreign serpents were believed to have been introduced into the Everglades when Hurricane Andrew hit Florida's coastline in August 1992. It was the most destructive hurricane to ever hit the state in terms of what would be damaged or destroyed. Among the chaos was a reptile breeding facility on the outskirts of the 'Glades, which collapsed in the wake of Andrew's powerful gusts and pelting rain.

When it did, a group of massive Burmese constrictors fled for the safety of the swamp where they would eventually populate and spread out.[135] Today, their growing presence has not only caused ecological damage but added a new level of fear for humans.

The Burmese python (*Python bivittatus*), which is native to Asia, can grow up to twenty feet in length and weigh as much as 150 pounds. They're nonvenomous, but they still have rows of razor sharp teeth that help them capture prey. Combined with their huge, articulating jaw, they can swallow prey many times larger than themselves. Some have been known to devour deer while others have even gone head-to-head with alligators. A video that shows a Burmese python strangling an alligator made the rounds on the internet a few years ago, illustrating the power and hunger of these fearless snakes. Because the female can lay up to a dozen eggs at a time, their population has exploded over the years. It's estimated by some that upwards of 100,000 Burmese pythons could be slithering around the Everglades today. Because they consume so much prey, they have literally disrupted the food chain for other apex predators like the Florida panther.

Human residents and visitors to the area are equally concerned due to the size and number of these snakes. If they prey on deer and alligators, they could just as easily swallow a human, especially if it's a child. It's a chilling thought, although such an incident has yet to occur in Florida. That doesn't mean it couldn't, however. In March of 2017, Akbar Salubiro, a twenty-five-year-old palm oil harvester from West Sulawesi, Indonesia, went missing. Three days later, authorities came across a twenty-three-foot-long Burmese python that had obviously ingested an extremely large meal. On a hunch the men apprehended the enormous snake, which was sluggish from the massive meal. When they sliced open its belly with a machete, they were horrified to find Mr. Salubiro's half-digested body inside![136]

The growing problem of Burmese pythons in the Everglades, primarily from an ecological standpoint, has been addressed by Florida officials. In 2017, the state hired twenty-five hunters whom they paid to capture and kill any of these pythons they could find.[137] The program resulted in hundreds of the snakes being harvested, with some of them as long as eighteen feet. Photos from the hunts posted online show various hunters holding up specimens, which illustrate how massive these muscular killing machines are. It's a "war" some believe is crucial to preserving the integrity of the Everglades' delicate ecosystem.

Tales of giant snakes certainly go hand in hand with swamps, and over the years the Everglades has spawned several. Rumors of impossibly large serpents living in the vast reaches of its marshes are hard to verify, but in the case of the Burmese python, perhaps rumors have finally manifested into disturbing reality.

Alongside tales of giant snakes are the persistent rumors of "alligator men" who supposedly inhabit the wilds of Florida's swamplands. They are said to be part human, part alligator, with the greenish, scaly body of a gator and the upper torso of a human. Various online articles claim sightings dating back to the 1700s, though no details are ever provided to back them up.[138] Nor have there been any modern eyewitness accounts to support the idea these bizarre creatures exist in the Everglades.

Rumors of the Everglades alligator people is most certainly the result of a laughable article that appeared in the November 9, 1993, issue of *Weekly World News*. The front page shows an eerie photo of a bizarre creature touted to be "Half-Man, Half-Alligator." In actuality, the photo is that of "Jake the Alligator Man," an infamous sideshow gaff that features a mummified-looking head and arms attached to a taxidermied alligator carcass. This clever creation is housed at Marsh's Free Museum in Long Beach, Washington, and was definitely not captured in the Everglades.

But alas, I shall not leave you in such defeat on the subject of Florida's reptilian humanoid case. There has been at least one intriguing report from another part of Florida that leaves me wondering if there just might be a grain of truth to this particular Sunshine State lore.

The report was sent to my colleague, Linda Godfrey, who included it in her excellent book, *American Monsters.*[ii] This first-hand, eyewitness story is very detailed and, by all accounts, credible. The witness in this case was an eighteen-year-old man who, at the time, was volunteering at a Florida paleontology museum while working toward his degrees in paleontology and zoology. According to the man (whose name has respectfully been kept from the public record), he saw a creature he could not identify while kayaking one of many canals of the swampy St. Johns River Delta in central Florida.[139] The witness explained that in April 2013, he was paddling through its brackish waters when something bumped his kayak. He didn't get a good look at the animal at first, so he took it to be a large alligator judging from a quick glimpse of a dark, scaly body and scutes rippling down its back. Concerned about the size, he quickly rowed to the nearest bank and got out of his kayak. As he stood on the sandy shore, he watched the animal navigate to the bank further down and crawl out of the water. Much to the witness's surprise, this was no mere gator. It had the general body characteristics of an alligator, but the head appeared "much taller vertically" than any alligator or crocodile he'd ever seen. It also had arms that were longer and "MUCH larger" than a normal crocodilian (the scientific classification that includes true crocodiles, alligators, and caimans) with "very obvious muscular tissue showing through the scales." Its legs, too, were broader and thicker and positioned "directly below the body rather than off to the sides like a reptile." Everything about this creature was disturbingly different. To make matters worse, it rose up on its hind legs and stood up! The witness said he could feel his blood run cold as

ii For the complete, detailed report as provided by the witness, refer to Linda's book *American Monsters* published by Tarcher Books.

this thing, which stood at least six to seven feet tall, turned and looked at him.

"It was completely unlike anything I'd ever seen, either living or in the fossil record," he stated. "I tried to scream but I couldn't even get it out of my throat."

The creature raised its elbows and made a deep, hissing sound. Before the witness could run, it turned and walked into the woods, first on two legs and then dropping back to all fours before disappearing into the brush. The startled witness quickly tied his kayak to a tree and ran to the nearest road. He did not dare get back in the water.

While this sighting would be enough to provide a lifetime of nightmares, it was not the only time the witness saw it. Later that night, he and a female friend (whom he decided not to tell what he'd seen earlier that day) were sleeping on his sailboat when he awoke at about 3:00 a.m. He could hear the sound of a slight, drizzly rain outside, and then suddenly, heard what he thought was a loud hiss.

"I peered out the porthole facing the canal entrance and I could see a figure in the dim light on the distant side of the canal," he said. "I nearly felt like I'd have a heart attack when I realized it was that 'thing' from earlier."

He immediately awakened his friend, who also looked out to see the creature. They watched for several horrified minutes as the thing maneuvered around the edge of the boat and even peered into the porthole, as if looking for something. Eventually, it backed up from the boat, turned, and lowered itself into the water until only its back and head were visible above the surface. Then it swam off into the mist, never to be seen again. As time has proven, a glimpse of the unknown is as fleeting as a ripple in the waters of a black lagoon.

Deep in the Everglades
(Photo by Tracy Robinson)

8

GREEN HELL

In his 1931 book, *Green Hell*, adventure writer Julian Duguid described the forests of the Amazon jungle as a "Green Hell." It was a place that appeared shady, cool, and beautiful when viewed by boat, yet fiendish, aloof, and powerfully callous when enveloped in its vast verdant interior.

"Under the shadow of its leaves I was tired, elated, thirsty, hungry and afraid," Duguid penned. "It hedged us in, dared us to venture through its bowers, coyly hid its water-holes from our sight, and loosed a covey of vampire bats when our animals could ill afford the blood."[140]

While the swamps of North America hold nary a green candle to the lush Amazon, it's not to say there aren't pockets on the continent where one could find suitable fiendish perils and callous pitfalls to threaten lives and scar the brain with visions of the unknown. Just consider the places we've covered so far. Certainly in any region where dense forestry meets standing water, there are going to be challenges—challenges that make our next few swamps both the embodiments of a greenish hell and a place where beauty can be deceiving.

Tate's Hell

With a name like Tate's Hell, I just had to investigate the history of this swamp. Not only does it have a menacing name, but it appears to be one of the most formidable patches of land in the state of Florida. Everywhere you look, the ageless, coastal bottoms of Tate's Hell are literally engulfed with waterways and woodlands, making it a truly rugged place if there ever was one.

Perhaps not surprisingly, I found an interesting backstory that hints at the dangers and mysteries living within.

Tate's Hell Swamp is located in the panhandle portion of northern Florida within the Tate's Hell State Forest, which comprises approximately 202,500 acres in Franklin and Liberty counties.[141] The terrain of the area is made up of a large patchwork of flatwoods and savannahs veined with an intricate web of creeks and bottoms whose muddy banks crawl with a wide array of beasts and insects. Plant life is rich here, boasting the unique dwarf cypress, whose sturdy limbs can live for more than a century.

According to legend, the forest and swamp were named after a man called Cebe Tate. Cebe was the son of Jebediah Tate who married a woman of Cherokee descent around the time of the Civil War. With the aid of a homestead grant, Jebediah purchased 160 acres of land near the town of Carrabelle, where he set up a small livestock farm to raise cattle.[142]

Over the next few years, the family prospered until Jebediah's wife contracted scarlet fever and died. Within a short time Jebediah and Cebe found themselves struggling to scratch out a living even though they had been successfully raising cattle and pigs, growing sugar cane, and harvesting pine oil on the side. Jebediah, being a highly superstitious man, believed this hardship was connected to the death of his Native American wife. So in an effort to restore prosperity, he made a pact with a local medicine man. In exchange for prosperity, Jebediah agreed to give the shaman and his people one pig each year and to stay out of their sacred cypress forest.

Things improved for Jebediah and his son until 1874, when Jeb decided not to give the medicine man his promised pig. This angered the shaman so much he promptly cursed the Tates, warning that they would see hardship like never before. Sure enough, within a short time Jebediah died of malaria, leaving Cebe alone. Soon the cattle begin to disappear into the swamp, the sugar cane wilted, and the pine oil dried up. Cebe tried to maintain the household by raising the pigs, but it was difficult. He eventually married a woman who had come from New York; however, ironically, she was Jewish and couldn't eat pork. When she complained of not having any beef, Cebe decided to take his hunting dogs into the sacred swamp to search for his rogue cows. Cebe's luck only got worse when his hunting dogs bolted after a panther and never returned. From there, Cebe became lost and stumbled through the humid hell confused, scared, and disoriented. Finally, the bewildered man sat down against the gnarled knee of an ancient dwarf cypress and fell into a troubled sleep.

Hours later Cebe was awakened by a sharp sting on his leg. He had been bitten by a venomous snake, which merely hissed and slithered off into the muck. Delirious from lack of food and the surging venom, Cebe got up and wandered through the swamp for another seven days, encountering strange animals and reeling from frightening visions. When he finally found his way out of the forest, he came upon two men who were walking down a road. He fell at their feet and muttered the haunting line: "My name is Cebe Tate and I just came through Hell." Cebe died shortly thereafter, and the swamp has been called Tate's Hell ever since.

Even with the best equipment and clothing, a weeklong journey into a swamp can be a potentially dangerous and scary experience, and in a place like Tate's Hell, undoubtedly deadly. While there's certainly no way to verify this legend, it's not the only one to walk out of those woods, so to speak.

In 2004, Bill Arnold was driving through Tate's Hell Forest on his way to St. George Island when a large, dark animal crossed the road on two legs.

"When I first saw it, I thought it must be a bear," Arnold told a reporter from the *Tallahassee Democrat*. "As I got closer and closer, I thought it might be a hunter. A big, hairy hunter."[143]

But as he watched it run toward the trees on the other side

of the road, he realized it was much too large to be a human. And much too hairy. He estimated the creature's height to be upward of eight feet with hair covering its entire body.

The thing glanced back at Arnold's approaching truck as it ran. Arnold noticed the animal had to turn its torso since it had no neck to speak of—only strong, powerful-looking muscles. After a few more seconds, the thing hit the treeline and disappeared into the brush.

As Arnold continued down the lonely road surrounded by miles of trees and murky water, he wondered just what *was* living in the heart of that spooky, strangely named swamp. His blood ran cold at the thought.

Twelve years later, another man asked himself the same thing. According to an interview conducted by my colleague David Lauer, a man named Virgil was driving toward the Bloody Bluff river landing in Tate's Hell Swamp one afternoon when he noticed a similar large figure on the side of the road ahead. As he approached, he realized it was some kind of hair-covered animal about six feet tall standing upright on two legs. The thing just stared at him as he drove by. Virgil was too frightened to stop, so he drove past it before turning around and speeding away from the area. It would be three years before he worked up the courage to return. Whatever lurked there in Tate's Hell, he did not want to encounter it again.

Gorilla Swamp and Devil's Dens

Whether the tale of Cebe Tate is the true reason for the swamp's name or not, surely this strange moniker was not chosen at random. As we have learned, location names are almost always based on some historical occurrence, superstition, or initial impression associated with the place. I found that to be the case with other swamps as well. For example, there's a tamarack wetland in central Michigan known as "Gorilla Swamp." Gorillas are definitely not indigenous to Michigan, so what would inspire such an odd name? Ironically, an article stowed away at the Folklore Archives at the Indiana University Library reveals a possible reason:

> *In Charlotte, Michigan, the whole town was upset one fall (1951) when there were reports of a strange monster loose in a swamp just outside of the town to the west. The people of the town couldn't identify it but one of the men decided it must be a gorilla because it stood on two feet. Because of this strange creature, seen on six or seven occasions by many different people, the area where it was seen is known as Gorilla Swamp.*[144]

An article from the July 14, 1950, edition of *The Michigan Daily* provides more details regarding the history of the location. The article states that residents south of Charlotte had reported "A strange beast—five feet high, hairy, with long forearms and a flesh-colored face ... hiding in the woods along M-29."[145] (At the time, M-29 went from Lansing through Charlotte to Marshall.)

The thing was first seen by a state highway patrolman, Jack Haley. According to Haley, "it came out of the driveway of a deserted home, crossed the highway, and fled into the darkness." Later that night a farmer named Alva Love saw something he couldn't identify in the swampy woods about one mile south of M-29. The witnesses said it could have been a baboon or gorilla, so authorities checked with officials of the Ringling Brothers and Barnum and Bailey Circus, which had coincidentally performed in Lansing on the same night. Not surprisingly, a circus representative said they hadn't lost any animals.

While the animal potentially fits the description of a chimpanzee (more so than a gorilla), it seems quite strange that any sort of great ape would be wandering through the woods of Michigan in the 1950s. While that doesn't mean it was something *unknown*, such as a Bigfoot, it is coincidental that in later years people would report sightings of a hairy, upright creature that most definitely fits the category of Bigfoot.

The most shocking of these encounters occurred in September 1974 near Marshall, Michigan. In this case, an X-ray machine repairman was traveling the backroads of Calhoun County when he observed a large, upright creature cross the road in front of his headlights.[146] It was covered in reddish hair and was at least seven feet tall. It quickly slipped into the shadows, leaving the man to question whether he had actually seen such a thing. The following week, he would have the answer.

As the man traveled the very same road at night, he noticed the same creature standing up ahead. It was holding what appeared to be roadkill. "It was smelling this thing and examining it very carefully," the witness explained to representatives of the Bigfoot Field Researchers Organization.

The witness said he stopped his truck in the middle of the road and watched the animal for approximately three minutes until it got up and started walking toward him. "When it got within ten feet I started backing up to keep a distance between me and it," he said. "It was dead-on in my headlights. This wasn't anyone wearing a costume."

The man continued to back his truck up slowly to maintain the distance between him and the frightening ape-like creature. After a few more feet, the thing simply turned and walked down into a ditch at the side of the road and into the woods.

"I stepped on the gas and got out of there … I never took that road again," he admitted. "It scared the living daylights out of me."

The man said he knew of at least one other witness who had seen a similar creature in the area, but that person would not talk to investigators. According to the witness, "he refuses to acknowledge this since he believes it was the devil's work."

The devil's work or not, the coincidence of a swamp named after a "gorilla" is certainly intriguing.

On the subject of hell and devils, it's also interesting to note that numerous geographic locations across North America have been named with some iteration of "Devil" as if to suggest an association with something dark and sinister. Places such as Devil's Island (Connecticut), Devil's Hollow (Massachusetts), Devil's Elbow (Missouri), Devil's Bathtub (Ohio), Devil's Garden (Utah), Devil's Tower (Wyoming)[iii], and Devil's Hall Trail (Texas) blend with so many Devil's Dens, Footprints, Playgrounds, Kitchens, and Backbones it's hard to even make a comprehensive list. Among these are several swamps bearing the name of the eternal evil one. I wasn't surprised to find these locations often have a proclivity for the paranormal. For example, Devil's Swamp of Thibodaux, Louisiana, is said to be haunted by the ghosts of buried slaves from Acadia Plantation as well as those of people murdered or killed on railroad tracks that cross a dusty side road near Schriever. Legend says if you park your car over the railroad tracks, it will stall, your windows will fog, and handprints will appear on the glass.[147] Elsewhere in the area, locals warn of a werewolf-like beast called the Rougarou (Roux-Ga-Roux), which roams the backwoods and swamplands.

Another Devil's Swamp, located in Scotlandville, Louisiana, is a large floodplain that consists of Devil's Swamp Lake and the swampy areas immediately adjoining the lake. Devil's Swamp was once a hauntingly beautiful freshwater wetland but has since become a dangerously toxic wasteland due to a hazardous chemicals disposal facility placed there in 1971.[148] Over the years, hunters have reported hearing strange explosions and machine-gun fire, which, along with the steady contamination of fish and game,

---

iii Devil's Tower in Wyoming - a distinctive, igneous rock formation known as a butte - was used as a plot element and film location for the 1977 movie, *Close Encounters of the Third Kind.*

make this a truly deadly environment.

In some cases, a devilish name can hint at the perils that may await within. Seven Devils Swamp, located near Monticello in far eastern Arkansas, is a maze of sloughs, creeks, and cypress thickets where it's easy to get lost. The swamp is made up of seven wide bodies of water off the main channel, which are intersected by so many tributaries it's hard to remember which ones have already been crossed while paddling its expanse. There are several stories to explain the origin of its name, all of them involving someone getting lost. The first of these tells of a fur trapper who, after getting lost for days in the maze, referred to its small lakes as "seven devils."[149] Another story claims the name was derived from locals who cursed the seven lakes as being "a devil to get to." Either way, travelers of old (without the benefit of compasses and GPS systems) were at risk of never returning from the winding waters of such a place, which may appear heavenly by day, but can quickly become a veritable hell by night.

Green Swamp / Devil's Creek (FL)

East of Tate's Hell, between Tampa and Orlando, Florida, lies an even larger expanse of treacherous terrain known as the Green Swamp. This 560,000-acre sprawl consists of flatlands, low ridges, and wetlands whose drainage creates the headwaters for four major rivers: the Withlacoochee, the Ocklawaha, the Hillsborough, and the Peace. The Green Swamp system sits in a giant basin and is one of the largest swamps in Florida. As with other murky woodlands, strange stories bubble to the surface on a regular basis.

In 1974, people in the area began to speak of a wild man who was supposedly living in the portion of the Green Swamp known as Devil's Creek. Hunters who braved its backwaters had caught glimpses of a feral-looking human near a pile of cracked armadillo shells that littered the ground. Police had even tried to track down the individual—whomever (or whatever) he or she was—but had no luck even with the use of bloodhounds. The best they'd gotten was a quick glimpse through the trees. They fired warning shots but to no avail.

By the spring of 1975, homes on the outskirts of the swamp were getting burglarized. Oddly enough, the thief was taking food such as cereal and cookies. Corn that had been left by game wardens to feed wild turkeys was also disappearing from the area. The police began to suspect the "wildman" was responsible so once again they set out for the area of Devil's Creek to search.

"On May 17, a posse descended on the Green Swamp to capture what they called the 'Green Swamp Wild Man,'" wrote a reporter from *The Orlando Sentinel*.[150] During the search they came across an island within the saw grass-soaked expanse of Devil's Creek, where they noticed a plume of smoke spiraling up from the trees. Deputies quickly made their way there and were surprised find a man—ragged, dirty, and primal looking—cooking by a fire. He bolted when he saw the posse, but the deputies tackled him and tried to calm him when he began to scream in a strange language. "It sounded like chanting," one of the lawmen told the *Sentinel* reporter.

As it turned out, the strange language was Mandarin Chinese, and the wild man was actually a Taiwanese refugee named Hu Tu-Mei. Hu had left his wife, four sons, and three daughters in Taipai, Taiwan, for the promise of the United States. However, Hu became homesick on the transport freighter and launched into a violent outrage. He was subdued by eight men and eventually taken to a Tampa hospital where he was to stay until authorities could fly him home. Before this could take place, however, Hu disappeared from the hospital and apparently fled into the Green Swamp where he subsequently survived for eight months.

When police locked him up for the suspected home burglaries, he continued to act erratically, telling an interpreter he believed the police were going to kill him. Two days after his arrest, Hu looped his belt through the bars of his cell in the Sumter County Jail and hanged himself. The ill-fated Taiwanese immigrant was gone, but the legend of the Green Swamp Wild Man lived on.

Elsewhere in the Green Swamp, traces of a ghost town known as Sturkey can be found hidden among the viny tendrils that claw at its remains. The ghost town is believed to have once been the site of a saw mill community, although there is little of its history on record. Whispers of ghosts and strange lights accompany mentions of the old town, but eyewitnesses are hard to come by.

Another landmark that should be haunted is the remains of the old Stewart Homestead. The place is nothing more than a rotted shack these days, but back in the early 1900s it was the cabin home of Isham Stewart (born 1860) and Sarah Stewart (born 1845), an honest, hardworking couple who had chosen to settle in what is now the Green Swamp Wildlife Management Area.

One night in May 1918, as the Stewarts were sleeping soundly, two men quietly entered their cabin through the front door. One of them crept over to the bed where the couple slept and raised a hefty ax above his head. Before the Stewarts could react, the man brought down the ax, killing them both in a bloody, violent act. After the screams and bed springs went silent, the men stole whatever cash the Stewarts had and made their escape into the dark swamp.

A week later a passerby noticed several grizzled vultures on the roof of the cabin, scratching and pecking as if trying to get inside. When he shooed them away and went inside, he was confronted by the horrible scene. A police investigation led to the arrest and conviction of Sarah's grandson, Josh Browning and his friend, Josh Tucker, on charges of murder.[151] It was one of the most heinous crimes the area had ever known.

The remains of the Stewarts were buried in a small graveyard behind the cabin, and a plaque was placed there as a tribute to these innocent victims and, perhaps, a reminder that humans may indeed be the most dangerous thing in a swamp.

Not to be outdone by its "hellish" counterpart to the west, Green Swamp also has a history of hairy hominid sightings. In fact, among Skunk Ape researchers, this lush, green wilderness is well-known for its compelling activity. Rumors of sightings go back to at least the 1950s with old-timers telling tales of ape-like things in and around the swamp. In 1974, a young man saw what he described as a "very large, upright monkey" in Polk County at the southern end of the Green Swamp. He was sitting outside with his father around sunset when they heard the sound of wood being chopped or "tapped" just behind their house.

"We stood up and looked to see if we could see anything behind the house when something that looked like a very large upright monkey crawled up one of the pine trees and jumped to another one," he reported. "It looked around for a moment and jumped down; what must have been 20 feet."[152]

The witness estimated the creature was about six or seven feet tall with brown hair covering its entire body. It was a "gorilla type" animal, although skinnier in build. He and his father were only about 250 feet from the tree, so there was no mistake what they had seen.

In 2004, Jennifer Ward said she was driving through the Green Swamp in northern Polk County when she caught sight of a haunting, human-like figure in a drainage ditch. It was covered in "dark hair or fur and had whitish rings around its eyes," she told reporters.[153] It raised its head as she approached.

"It looked like it was doing something," Ward said. "Whenever it saw me, it probably took on the facial expression I had on because I was dumbfounded. It just watched me as I drove by."

Ward had never placed much stock in the reality of Florida's alleged Skunk Ape, but now she was forced to rethink her position. "I didn't really think it existed, but I'm convinced now," she admitted.

In 2008, a hunter in Polk County was watching for deer one evening when he observed a five-to-six-foot-tall animal eating persimmons from a tree.[154] He initially thought it was a bear, but after he watched it for several minutes, the animal stood up and walked off on two legs. It walked for approximately forty yards before it disappeared into the thick undergrowth. Upon observing the animal's gait and movements, the hunter was convinced it was *not* a bear.

Sometimes in these swampy scenarios, it's what you hear—or don't hear—that's spooky. My friend and fellow author, Robert Robinson, was with his son in the Devil's Creek section of the Green Swamp several years ago when they heard something splashing in the darkness. It sounded as if it was walking on two legs, though they were sure no other people were around. Earlier in the night they'd noticed a strange stillness, which seemed unusual for such a vibrant swamp. Now something definitely did not seem right. As soon as they heard the unseen thing move, Rob noticed the insects and other animals went completely silent. As he and his son listened in the darkness, Rob wondered what was out there. When it suddenly stopped walking, he got a distinct and "overpowering" feeling that someone—or some*thing*—was watching him.

"I took out my night-vision goggles and looked in the direction of the splashing," Robinson recalled. "Then I saw them: large, glowing eyes staring right at me!"[155] While he couldn't be sure it was one of Florida's infamous Skunk Apes, it was enough to send icy chills down his spine.

In the winter of 2011, a man was camping with his son in

the West Tract of the Green Swamp Wilderness Preserve when they were awakened at 2:00 a.m. by a haunting, "whooping, screaming, howl."[156] As an experienced outdoorsman, he knew it wasn't a coyote or a wildcat, but was unsure just what kind of animal it could have been. It was unlike anything he'd ever heard.

Father and son lay there for several minutes listening intently in the darkness, but the howl did not repeat. Just when their nerves began to calm, they heard a strange whistling noise moving around the perimeter of their camp. "It was not like a bird; it was almost like a human whistling a tune but much louder," the man recalled. Their blood ran cold as the sound continued in long, drawn-out whistles followed by a pause. Something strange was definitely going on, but they didn't dare venture out of their tent to investigate.

After the whistling stopped, the men eventually drifted back to sleep. An hour later, however, the father awoke for some reason and opened his eyes. Something was creeping around outside their tent. In the moonlight, he could see the silhouette of a large figure as it cast a shadow on the wall of the tent. He couldn't discern very many characteristics, but was clear it was something walking upright. Needless to say, the campers did not remain in the Green Swamp for a second night.

It's impossible to say what was making the noise or what was walking around the tent, but at least the father and son lived to tell the story. Sometimes people never make it back once they venture into a sinister swamp. On November 24, 2004, Shirley Huff returned home from work in the evening to find her husband, Charles, gone.[157] She was aware he planned to go hunting in the Green Swamp the following day, but by the looks of his missing Ruger M77 rifle, he must have gone scouting a day early, even though she explicitly told him not to go into the swamp alone. Shirley did not understand why he set out some chicken to thaw for the evening's meal if he hadn't planned on returning in time to cook it.

Worried, Shirley called her daughters, but neither had heard from Charles. When he hadn't returned by midnight, Shirley's daughter, Terry Griffin, called the authorities.

The next day (Thanksgiving morning, no less) a Polk County sheriff's deputy came to the house and met with Shirley and several other members of the family. One of Shirley's son-in-laws, Todd Tharrington, suggested they look at a spot in the Green Swamp Wildlife Management Area where he and Charles had once fished. When Tharrington led authorities to the location, they found Charles's Mazda truck but no sign of Charles himself. A quick search of the thickly wooded area proved fruitless.

The next day, a more official search was organized. This included deputies from the Polk and Sumter sheriffs' offices, as well as three trained rescue dogs. The dogs were given samples of Charles's clothing to learn the scent, but were ultimately unsuccessful in locating him because a sudden storm the night before had essentially washed away whatever trace had remained of the man.

At one point, approximately two hundred searchers lined up shoulder to shoulder and moved methodically through the swampy woods using machetes to cut their way. It was so thick, Lieutenant George Wilson of the Florida Fish and Wildlife Conservation Commission noted: "visibility was often limited to a few feet." Wilson said searchers on foot scoured an area extending two miles in all directions from Huff's truck. They also combed the area on horseback and in all-terrain vehicles as well as by air using helicopters equipped with sophisticated sensors. All of it was to no avail.

After ten days of exhaustive searching, the Huff family conceded to call off the search. Not a single thing had been found: no footprints, scent trails, or any other clues. It was as if Charles had simply walked into the swamp and disappeared from the face of the earth. Some suspected foul play, but either way, no trace of Charles Huff was ever found.

The foreboding Green Swamp of Florida (Photo by Adam Davies)

Green Swamp / Big Swamp (NC)

While the Green Swamp of North Carolina isn't nearly as large as its Florida counterpart, it has some interesting qualities and a beastly tale that plants it firmly within the shaded waters of our sinister pursuit.

Located in the heart of North Carolina's Brunswick County, the Green Swamp offers 15,000 acres of exceptional ecology, where longleaf pine savanna forests and pocosin bogs create a unique habitat that is home to a number of rare carnivorous plant species."[158] The most famous of these is the *Dionaea muscipula*, or as it's more dramatically known, the Venus flytrap. The bog's wet, acidic soil (made up of a nitrogen-poor mixture of peat and sand) does not supply enough nutrients for the typical array of swamp flora, so carnivorous plants do well because they are able to take nutrients from other sources. The Venus flytrap is technically *insectivorous*, since it survives by solely eating insects who are attracted to its sweet-smelling nectar and bright-red leaves. When an insect lands between these mouth-like leaves and disturbs at least two of six "trigger hairs," the mouth snaps shut to secure the meal. It then takes around ten days for the plant to break down and digest the enzymes from the insect, leaving only a dry exoskeleton to be blown away by the wind when the mouth reopens.

When I was young, I was enthralled by the Venus flytrap. Advertising in the back of comic books offered these "mysterious creations which actually eat raw beef" for the mere price of one dollar plus twenty-five cents postage. I just knew my friends and family would be impressed if I were to get one and drop a steak in its mouth. We would watch its mouth snap viciously shut!

This type of enticing advertising and commercial harvesting resulted in the Venus flytrap becoming an endangered plant species. The flytrap can only grow naturally in a one-hundred-mile area of southern North Carolina and northern South Carolina, so its existence was easily threatened. Nowadays, the preservation of the Green Swamp has become a key ingredient in the plant's survival.

In addition to the legendary flytrap, the Green Swamp hosts several other insectivorous plants including sundews, butterwort, and four varieties of the pitcher plant. It also nurtures a wide variety of orchids and wildflowers that provide a contrasting pop of color to the murky green vista.

This foray into bloodsucking plants is not only to highlight the uniqueness of the Green Swamp, but to point out a bit of irony. While the Green Swamp isn't necessarily the spookiest swamp in a visual sense, it is part of a network of coastal swamps infamous for being the home of a bloodsucking, carnivorous mystery monster the newspapers dubbed the "Vampire Beast!"

The story started on the night of December 31, 1953, when something killed two dogs belonging to Johnny Vause, a resident of the small mill town of Bladenboro, North Carolina. He was shocked by what he discovered.

> *There was blood all over the porch, big puddles of it. And there was a pool of saliva on the porch. It killed one dog at 10:30 and left it lying there. My dad wrapped the dog up in a blanket. That thing came back and got that dog and nobody's seen the dog since. At 1:30 in the morning, it came back and killed the other dog and took it off. We found it three days later in a hedgerow. The top of one of the dog's heads was torn off and its body was crushed and wet, like it had been in that thing's mouth. The other dog's lower jaw was torn off.*[159]

The following night two more dogs were killed at a farm in Bladenboro. According to the horrified owner, Woodie Storm, his pets were "eaten up."

On the night of January 2, 1954, yet another dog suffered the same fate, this time belonging to a farmer by the name of Gary Callahan. Two more were found dead in the Bladenboro area on January 3. In this case one of the dog's jawbones was "smashed," and its ear was gnawed off, while both dogs' tongues were "chewed out." By now local Chief of Police, Roy Fores, was so concerned he ordered an autopsy on one of the dogs in an attempt to identify what might have killed them. Fores reported that "there wasn't more than two or three drops of blood in him," leading to speculation that whatever was doing the killing was literally drinking the blood of its victims.

No one had seen the culprit in the act of killing the dogs,

but some residents caught glimpses of an animal they believed might be responsible. A man named Malcolm Frank said he saw a shadowy creature cross the street. He said it was "about four and a half feet long, bushy, and resembling either a bear or a panther." On January 3, James Pittman heard a noise outside his home like a "baby crying." When he went outside to investigate, he saw some kind of animal moving through the bushes. Though he never got a good look at it, he figured it had to be large, weighing in the vicinity of 150 pounds.

The following evening, Lloyd Clemmons was sitting with his wife in their living room when they heard their dogs begin to bark. "I glanced out the window and saw this thing," he told a news reporter. "It had me plumb spellbound. It was about 20 inches high [with] a long tail, about 14 inches. The color of it was dark. It had a face exactly like a cat, only I ain't ever seen a cat that big. It was walking around stealthy, sneaky, moving about trying to get to [my dogs]. I jumped for my shotgun and loaded it and went out to shoot it, but it moved into the darkness right away and I couldn't find him again."[160]

Soon, the town of Bladenboro become the focal point of a monster hunt. Articles about the gruesome dog deaths published in local and surrounding newspapers lured in carloads of amateur hunters ready to put an end the unseen predator's reign of terror.

Bladenboro is located in the swampy coastal region of North Carolina just west of the famed Bermuda Triangle, where it's flanked by a number of swamps. This includes Green Swamp and Red Hill Swamp to the southeast and Big Swamp to the north, all likely haunts for whatever might be wreaking havoc in Bladenboro. Local residents were obviously concerned for the safety of their pets and for themselves, although thus far the beast had not threatened any people. That would change, however, on the night of January 5. According to a news article with the dramatic title "'Vampire' Charges Woman," a Mrs. C. E. Kinlaw of Bladenboro was rushed by a "large marauding cat" when she walked into her front yard to find out why her dogs were whimpering. She told reporters: "It raced from three doors down the dirt street in front of her house to a few feet from her porch, then turned back when she screamed and her husband rushed out." The Kinlaws watched in horror as it fled into the nearby swamp.

Once the beast was out of sight, the Kinlaws called the police to report the incident. When Chief Fores arrived at the scene, he discovered large tracks with claw impressions along the dirt road in front of their home. The tracks were described as being "about half the size of a man's hand, and resembling either a dog or cat's print."[161] Theories as to what the beast might be ranged from a wildcat to a wild dog, with most bets laid on it being a "maddened panther."[162] The only problem was feline prints do not typically register claw impressions since cats have retractable claws, not to mention game authorities claimed there were no panthers (cougars) living in North Carolina at the time. The last verified sighting of a cougar was near the town of Highlands in 1905.[163] This was a conundrum since witnesses described it as being cat-like, yet the prints and data did not lend much support to it being felid.

Whatever this thing was—felid, canid, or otherwise—it appeared to be hiding out in the overgrown reaches of the swamp where it could emerge unseen at night to terrorize the surrounding communities. Concerned that its next victim might be a person, Fores decided to organize an official posse to hunt down the thing newspapers were now referring to as the "Vampire Beast," "Bleeder Beast," or "Beast of Bladenboro."

On January 6, Fores, along with a group of fifty to sixty men (comprised of deputies and armed citizens from Bladenboro and beyond) and four tracking dogs, plunged into the swamp and surrounding thickets to search for the animal. The men searched for hours, combing every possible acre, but never got eyes on the

Beast. The only evidence they found was more footprints. Judging from the size of the tracks, there appeared to be two beasts, one larger than the other.

Fores may not have seen the Beast, but it was apparently close by. He said around 1:30 a.m. he and another man were standing in Bladenboro when they heard a dog cry out in pain. Fores said he "could tell the animal was going, or being dragged into dense everglade growths bordering the houses."[164]

Over the next week as many as five hundred hunters scoured the swampy region in search of the Vampire Beast. However, it remained elusive. The next confirmed sighting was on January 11 when it crossed the road in front of two vehicles. The witnesses—six in all— described it to Chief Fores as being about "four feet long and two feet high" with a long tail and a large head with "runty-looking" ears.[165]

In response to this latest sighting, which was near what the locals called Big Swamp, a clever hunter named Luther Davis quickly set up a trap designed to catch large predators in the murky bog just off the road. Sure enough, when he checked the trap the next morning it held a good-sized bobcat. Davis said the animal was "still scrappy," so he had to shoot it before he could remove it from the enclosure.[166] The cat measured thirty inches long and weighed approximately thirty-five pounds, and it had a stumpy tail. This was considerably smaller than what witnesses described, and its tail was far too short, but it was good enough for Mayor W. G. Fussell of Bladenboro to proclaim the Beast had been slain. When Luther Davis displayed his trophy in town, the locals celebrated the victory.

The underwhelming bobcat, however, was not the only suspect. An auto parts dealer from nearby Lumberton said he'd owned a large dog that was part hound and part German shepherd. The dog once patrolled his place of business but would not stay in the enclosure with a six-foot fence, so he was forced to give it away to "an Indian boy who lives on the edge of Big Swamp."[167] The man felt the dog could have been responsible for the rampage, although it seems unlikely a dog would have done what the Beast of Bladenboro did, nor does it fit the "cat-like" descriptions.

Fears Return Over 'Beast Of Bladenboro'

LUMBERTON, N.C., Dec. 15 (AP) —The "Beast of Bladenboro" may be on the prowl again.

Last night five pigs and three chickens were killed on the K. M. Biggs farm here, giving rise to the fear that the infamous nocturnal wanderer is back.

A mysterious animal last year terrorized Bladenboro for days and groups of men, armed with guns, searched nightly to no avail.

The pigs were mutilated and four had crushed skulls. The chickens were decapitated. No blood was evident, indicating the killer employed the same blood - sucking traits as the Bladenboro beast.

Several tracks were found in the area which Biggs said measured four inches in length.

One of the many "Beast of Bladenboro" news articles (Asheville Citizen Times – December 16, 1954)

The night after Davis killed the bobcat, Bruce Soles was driving on the highway near Bladenboro when he struck and killed a "leopard-like" animal. This animal, believed by some to be an ocelot, stood about two feet high and weighed between seventy-five and ninety pounds.[168] It also had an eight-inch-long tail. This animal matched witness descriptions far better than the bobcat, which went further in reassuring the people of Bladenboro that perhaps the perpetrator was finally dead.

In the weeks and months that followed, no more pets turned up dead, nor did anyone spot the Vampire Beast skulking around. The short burst of terror, which inspired an unprecedented amount of news coverage and frenzy, was apparently over. In time, the memory faded, and people gradually went back to the regularity of their lives. But those who lived on the edge of the swamp could not completely forget the thing that once prowled there. At the end of the day, when the sun began to set in the bottoms, they always glanced twice at the darkening shadows forming at its edge. Something could still be out there; watching; waiting; ready to strike again when the urge becomes too great. The swamp is the keeper of secrets, and among them, the true identity of the infamous Beast of Bladenboro.

9

THE CADDO TRIANGLE

At the northern end of Louisiana, where the sportsman's paradise meets Texas and Arkansas, lies a region of waterways and woodlands I call the *Caddo Triangle*. The greater area is often referred to by locals as the "Ark-La-Tex," but for my purposes I prefer something more dramatic and geographically focused to reflect the history of strange encounters that have taken place there over the years.

The geometric shape and its naming draw obvious similarities to the Bermuda and Bridgewater triangles, although the range of phenomena exhibited within the Caddo Triangle is more limited in scope. I suppose it's more of a southern version where Indian legends meet modern sightings of hairy, ape-like creatures against a backdrop of double-barreled shotguns, moonshine, and Cajun spices. It may not include the compass-needle-breaking powers of the famed Bermuda Triangle or the vast paranormal phenomena of its Bridgewater counterpart, but you would still be ill-advised to enter its off-road domain without sufficient fortitude and preparation.

The Caddo Triangle, as I have defined, is anchored at three points, each of which is significant to both the phenomenon of cryptids and the independent cinema that has been birthed from these regional tales. The points are Caddo Lake on the west (Texas), Bayou Bodcau on the east (Louisiana), and Mercer Bayou to the north (Arkansas). Within this triangle, miles upon miles of scenically beautiful and haunting swampscapes spread out among thick forests of cypress and pine like a mixture of sweet tea and greenery. The area is both remote and accessible, blending the best of backcountry life with the recreational desires of countless visitors. By all appearances, scenic destinations within the triangle exemplify the best of what the Ark-La-Tex has to offer, yet behind its timeless wall of biome beauty lurks a southern mystery that some may find rather unsettling.

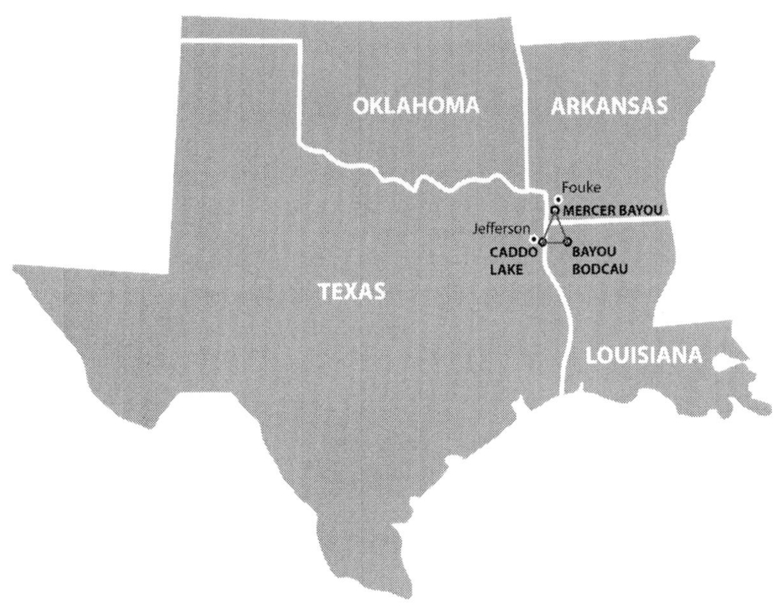

The Caddo Triangle

Bayou Bodcau

In the long list of Louisiana swamps, Bayou Bodcau may seem rather mundane, yet it stands out as one of the largest remaining expanses of bottomland hardwood habitat in the northern portion of the state. Not to mention, it's been the source of some rather eerie tales, some of which have even inspired Louisiana movie culture.

The whole of Bayou Bodcau is comprised of 43,000 acres

of alluvial wetlands in the floodplain between the Bodcau Dam (south of Sarepta) and the Red River to the west.[169] The bayou channel runs a long, winding path of more than thirty miles, giving it a sort of serpentine shape. This region was originally home to the Caddo Indians, whose villages dotted the landscape more than 5,000 years ago. The bayou was not only used as a water source, but also as an avenue for travel by canoe or "dugout." By the late 1800s, European settlers had moved in to establish their own communities and farms, with corn and cotton being the staple crops.

Nowadays, the Bayou Bodcau Reservoir and Bayou Bodcau State Wildlife Management Area are popular spots for outdoor recreation, yet these bottoms still elicit an eerie chill when the sun goes down. The nature of its thick, flooded forestry makes you feel as though you've left the modern world for something our ancestors would have been familiar with all those years ago.

I first heard of Bayou Bodcau while researching the history of a Bigfoot-themed movie that was shot near Oil City, Louisiana, in 1976. The movie, titled *Creature from Black Lake*, was produced by a Louisiana filmmaker who was attempting to cash in on the popularity of *The Legend of Boggy Creek*, a similar movie made in Arkansas and released in 1972. While reading some articles about the making of *Creature from Black Lake*, one of the producers noted that it was inspired by sightings of a strange, hairy creature in the black bottoms of Bayou Bodcau. I had always assumed *Creature from Black* Lake was solely motivated by *The Legend of Boggy Creek,* which was in turn inspired by eyewitness accounts of a Bigfoot-like creature said to live near the small town of Fouke, Arkansas, some forty miles northwest of Bodcau. Upon reading this intriguing tidbit about Bayou Bodcau, I set out to learn more about its darker side.

One of the first stories I came across dates back to 1958. On July 29 of that year, R.E. Omberg and her brother Olie Robinson were fishing at Bodcau Dam when they spotted a dark, snake-looking creature wriggling through the brushy water headed right toward them. Without much thought, Robinson grabbed their cloth fish net and scooped the thing out of the water.[170]

Upon examination, they weren't sure if it was a snake, lizard, or something else. It was about seven inches long with small legs (or arms), four toes, and leafy-like ears that almost looked like horns. Figuring it was worth keeping, Robinson threw it into the bucket where they'd been keeping their day's catch of carp and gaspergou. Fifteen minutes later, they noticed all the fish were dead and floating on their backs. The snake-thing, however, was still very much alive and swimming peacefully in the water.

The weird incident caused Mrs. Omberg to reflect on other strangeness going on at Bodcau. Several times she had come out in the morning to fish only to find hundreds of them floating stomach-up in the water. Olie himself had seen a "big bass leap into the air and, before he could cast, seeing the fish quiver, and flop over dead." Other fisherman, too, mentioned they'd seen fish dying in droves over the last a decade. Bones often littered the banks of the boggy bayou.

Even stranger, several old-timers recalled a time around 1928, before the dam was built, when some cattle waded into the bayou. They, too, died—keeling over into the black water as if they'd been killed instantly. Even worse, two young boys had inexplicably drowned while swimming in the bayou a few years earlier. By all accounts the boys were both exceptional swimmers, so no one could figure out how this happened. Theories led to tales of a "monstrous sea serpent" some thought may have found its way into Bodcau.

The slithery thing Robinson and Omberg had caught was far too small to be a "sea serpent," but it was definitely odd. They had seen most everything the wetlands had to offer, and this was something they'd never encountered. Perhaps, they thought, it was an electric eel? If a family of these things were living in Bodcau, then it might explain what was killing the fish, cattle, and perhaps the boys—electrocution!

Omberg and Robinson kept the thing alive as they pored over encyclopedias and almanacs trying to identify it. When they dropped a minnow in the bucket, it was killed instantly when the thing lashed its tail. "It seemed to grow black when it became angry," they remarked.

Eventually, Omberg reached out to the local college biology department, who sent one of its staff, Dr. Mary Warters, to examine the creature. Anticipation was high, but her conclusion was less than groundbreaking. After some deliberation, Warters concluded it was a Texas Dwarf Siren, a type of salamander. Though it was extremely rare to catch one, it did not possess any sort of electrical charge, ruling out the theory that it could be responsible for the strange deaths. Warters and others theorized the fish in Bodcau had died of heat exposure from the hot summer sun. They could not explain the rumor of cattle dying in the water, however.

Omberg and Robinson accepted the finding, but were not completely convinced something unknown wasn't amiss in the dark waters of the bayou. Robinson had seen bass quiver and die right before his eyes, appearing very much like they'd been "shocked." As he continued to fish the dam, he was careful not to wade too far into the water. Bayou Bodcau could yet hold a sinister secret.

In the early 1970s, a rash of reports out of the Bodcau area suggested something monstrous could indeed be stalking its backwaters. The first comes from 1971. On a cool November morning of that year, a man was squirrel hunting among the cypress trees about two miles from his home on Bayou Bodcau when he heard dogs running something through the woods. Figuring it was a deer, he switched from squirrel shot to buckshot in his 12-gauge shotgun.

"I then saw what I thought was a person break through some brush and slide down the bank almost to the water," he reported. "It then crawled back up the bank and turned and looked my way."[171]

The man was completely shocked. It was some kind of upright creature with reddish-brown hair covering its body (about the length of deer hair). It stood approximately six to six-and-a-half feet tall and looked "incredibly human-like judging from its nose, eyes, and ears."

The creature lingered only a few seconds before it "turned north and jogged up the creek until it was out of sight." The dogs that had been chasing it never emerged from the brush, so the hunter never saw them.

The following day, the man told his father what he'd seen. His father asked the age-old question in regard to Bigfoot-type encounters with hunters: "Why didn't you shoot it?" The witness echoed the sentiments of many others who have come face-to-face with such a being: "I told him it looked too much like a man."

Sometime around 1973, Joseph Barber was sitting on a makeshift deer stand in the Bodcau woods when he heard something crunching through the leaves. By the sound of the footsteps, he assumed it was another hunter, although he'd rarely seen anyone else in that part of the woods. Barber was agitated since he thought it might scare the deer away. The sun was just starting to set, and he was positioned on a game trail that was always plentiful with wildlife.

The crunching would stop for several moments before resuming. Whatever it was seemed to be coming toward his tree stand. Barber fully expected a camouflaged hunter to emerge from the trees, but that wasn't the case.

"I was sitting there kind of annoyed when all of sudden I saw a dark figure moving just behind a cluster of trees," Barber told me in an interview. "It was walking upright, but the closer it got the more I could say it wasn't a man."

The figure never fully emerged from the trees, but passed close enough for Barber to see it was covered in dark hair or fur, and stood approximately six to seven feet tall. Its arms hung somewhat lower than a human as it walked, sort of slouching slightly. Barber could only make out the profile of its face, which appeared to have a "large, smashed-down nose" and a "protruding jaw."

The hunter's reaction quickly shifted from being annoyed to being afraid.

"I just sat there kind of fixed as I watched it disappear again into the trees," Barber explained. "After I knew it was long gone, I got out of the stand and ran as fast as I could to my truck. The whole time I was worried it would hear me and come after me."

The reports of a hairy, man-like thing coming out of Bodcau were enough to catch the attention of Louisiana filmmaker, Jim McCullough, Sr., and producer Dr. W. Lew Ryder who were looking to cash in on the popularity of *The Legend of Boggy Creek*, which had been booming at the box office since its release in 1972. *The Legend of Boggy Creek*, directed by Charles B. Pierce, was an independently made film based on true accounts of a similar hairy creature stalking the bottoms of southwest Arkansas. McCullough and Ryder figured they could do the same with their own seminal creature from Louisiana.

The resulting movie was *Creature from Black Lake* released in 1976. Like *Boggy Creek, Creature* was funded and filmed locally and distributed through HowCo International. In the film two grad students from the University of Chicago become interested in Bigfoot. When they hear of a recent sighting from the South—in which an old-timer saw his friend dragged into the bayou by a hairy, man-like creature—the students decide to head that way and spend their summer break looking for the creature. They arrive in Oil City (an actual town) eager to talk to the locals but are greeted with silence and hostility regarding their research. Ignoring an order by the sheriff to leave, they keep up the search that eventually incurs the wrath of an angry man-ape.

Much of the movie's entertainment value is due to the performance of the two grads, Rives and Pahoo, played by TV veterans John David Carson (*CHiPs*) and Dennis Fimple (*The Dukes of Hazard*), and the memorable Jack Elam (*Rawhide*, *Gunsmoke*, etc.). It also benefits from the film locations, including the town of Oil City and Caddo Lake, a hauntingly picturesque bayou-lake on the border of Louisiana and Texas a mere twenty-five miles from Bayou Bodcau itself. The swamp scenery is spooky and the action entertaining enough to create a memorable film for its time. The fact that it's inspired by actual reports of an unknown swamp creature makes it all the more interesting.

The author exploring the swamps of Louisiana in 2011 (Photo by Tom Shirley)

Caddo Lake / Big Cypress Bayou

The first time I explored the shadowed coves of Caddo Lake, I was absolutely enthralled. I was there with my late friend, Tom Shirley, for a weekend of camping and exploration. We had heard the legends and watched *Creature from Black Lake* many times, so in some ways it was hauntingly familiar. But nothing could truly compare to being there in person.

I remember marveling at the gray ghosts of Spanish moss swaying from the cypress trees as we floated along in our canoe. I alternately paddled as Tom did the same, stopping occasionally to listen to the chorus of insects and frogs that were warming up for the night's performance. Among them, birds chirped and called to signal the end of the day. Somewhere in the distance a bull alligator bellowed. He sounded big, and I was glad he wasn't swimming in our slough.

Caddo Lake is one of the most impressive examples of what I would call a primordial paradise. Its swampy waters are filled with a countless array of living things, from microscopic plants to the aforementioned bull gators. On the surface—which is a glistening sheen of black tea—patches of peat form small, drifting islands while bright green duckweed and salvinia attempt to crowd them out. Clusters of ancient cypress rise above as if standing guard over their timeless domain. Beneath them, stark white herons fish with bright orange beaks, and water snakes lie in wait, unseen in the shadows of reeds and cypress knees lining the jagged edges of the coves. It's like a scene from a prehistoric film I'd watched as a kid; a place I would have loved to go then and a place I have returned to many times now.

Caddo Lake and its network of associated bayou channels are located at the edge of East Texas and West Louisiana, where it straddles the border in equal parts. Caddo is one of the only natural lakes in Texas and is thought to have been formed by either the

New Madrid earthquakes of 1811–1812 or as a result of a huge logjam in the Red River, which in the early 1800s forced enough water into Big Cypress Bayou to create the lake. The resulting wetlands system is comprised of about 26,800 acres of cypress swamp with an average depth of around nine feet. The state park commission has mapped an astounding forty-two miles of "boat roads" to guide visitors through Caddo's endless maze of channels.[172]

Wildlife in the area is plentiful, boasting upward of 240 bird species, along with deer, raccoon, beaver, mink, nutria, hogs, squirrel, armadillo, frogs, turtles, snakes, gators, and some say, the Caddo Creature.

Legends of strange things in the area date back to the first native inhabitants. The Caddo Indian tribe, for which the lake was named, spoke of a race of large beings who inhabited the woods of the Ark-La-Tex. According to Kathy Strain, archaeologist and author of *Giants, Cannibals & Monsters: Bigfoot in Native Culture*, they referred to them as the *ha'yacatsi,* which translates to "lost giants."

In modern times, sightings of large, hairy creatures in the backwoods of Caddo Lake and its four watersheds (Little Cypress Bayou, Big Cypress Bayou, Black Cypress Bayou, and Jeems Bayou) have persisted for years. One of the first on record was publicized by *The Longview News Journal.* In the article, Richard Eason said he was working as a conductor for the T&P Railroad.[173] On a cold November night in 1927, he was conducting the train through rural Marion County, Texas (which holds much of Caddo Lake) when he stopped at a telephone house to call ahead.[iv] When Eason opened the door to the phone house, he caught a glimpse of something standing in the flickering firebox light of the train's oil-burning engine. He said it appeared to be "a giant ape or a gorilla … standing on its back feet with its arms upraised and teeth

iv Prior to the installation of modern signal and centralized traffic control systems, all communications on the line had to be done by phones stationed along the tracks.

bared."

Eason was so frightened he immediately retreated back to the engine where he told the engineer and fireman what he'd seen. Not surprisingly, neither of the men wanted to get off the train to investigate.

On August 20, 1965, thirteen-year-old Johnny Maples was walking on a rural road in Marion County when a "large hairy man or beast" emerged from the woods, jumped a fence, and started toward him. Maples panicked and started running.[174]

"I ran as hard and fast as I could, but he kept up with me and he wasn't running, either, just sort of walking along behind me," Maples told a reporter from the *Marshall News Messenger*. The boy kept running, all the while looking back to see the hairy beast in pursuit. "The last time I turned around the beast had gone off the road and disappeared into the woods," he explained. "I could hear him moving around but I didn't see him again."

A neighbor eventually drove by in a car and gave Johnny a ride home. When the boy told the story to his mother (who noted her son was in a "state of shock"), she immediately called the Marion County Sheriff's Office. A deputy was sent to the scene, but he could find no evidence of the alleged beast. Maples described it as a seven-foot-tall ape with long black hair all over its body except for the face, stomach, and palms of its hands, which, he noted, "hung down below his knees."

Shortly after the Maples's incident, a couple walking in the nearby Old Foundry Cemetery heard a blood-chilling scream from the woods. The next day they found a set of large, unidentified animal tracks outside the cemetery gates. The prints were believed to have been made by the same creature, which the newspaper dubbed the "Marion County Monster."

The events quickly brewed up a "monster hunt" conducted by locals and outsiders. In a 1965 *United Press International* article titled "Town Fed Up With Monster Hunters," Sheriff Luke

Walker of Jefferson, Texas, told a reporter that Bigfoot hunters from three states had overrun his small town since the news of Maples's encounter had spread.[175]

Charles Fason saw a similar beast in the very heart of the Caddo swampland. Fason grew up on the west side of Caddo Lake, and as a boy he and his brother spent countless hours exploring its murky backwaters. They had their own boat and even constructed a treehouse where Big Cypress Bayou joins the main lake channel (in an area known as Devil's Elbow) to use for hunting and overnight fishing trips. One night in the summer of 1969, the Fasons were sleeping in their treehouse when Charles was awakened by noises around midnight. He figured it was the usual "night critters" sniffing around but decided to have a look anyway. As he peered between wooden slats of the crude treehouse wall, he was shocked to see a tall, upright animal standing a short distance away. Charles quickly awakened his brother.

"We're sitting there looking at this thing, and it started moving towards us," Fason told me in an interview. It walked to where they had thrown some leftovers from dinner and reached down to scoop them up. "Then it looked right directly back at us."

For a few tense moments the boys remained frozen, wondering what the animal would do now that it was aware of their presence. But after a few moments, it took off into the woods at an incredible speed.

"For something this big to move that fast was unbelievable," Fason recalled. "We could hear limbs snapping as it ran. Needless to say I didn't sleep the rest of the night. We were watching to see if it came back, but it never did."

The next day the boys found several man-like footprints left by the creature in the soft mud. They did not have a ruler, but they compared the impressions to their own feet. Fason estimates the creature's foot was at least sixteen inches. Judging by the height of the treehouse and the position where the creature was standing,

Fason estimated it must have stood over seven feet tall.

Fason noted the creature had not made any verbal noises, although he and his brother had heard unexplained high-pitched howls in the area on several other occasions. These mysterious calls did not come from any animal or bird they were familiar with, and after their sighting, he believed the unidentified howls may have been connected to the strange animal. The swamp could get pretty spooky at night, and this only made it spookier.

In the fall of 1987, a man was hunting along Big Cypress Bayou (not far from the Fason boys' treehouse) when he also observed a strange animal. According to a report filed with the Bigfoot Field Researchers Organization, he was in his deer stand around mid-afternoon when he noticed a dark figure moving approximately fifty yards away.[176] It stood up from a crouched position in the shallow, murky water of the bayou. The animal "appeared to be six feet tall, covered with hair from head to toe." As the hunter watched, the thing moved its head from side to side, as if looking for something. Then, after about two minutes, it simply turned and walked into the woods. The experience was so unnerving, the hunter decided to leave the area as quickly as he could rather than pursue the creature.

Around the same time, two men had an equally disturbing experience at the Jeems Bayou watershed on the north end of Caddo Lake. According to Roger Murray—who contacted me a few years ago—his friend Tommy had a camp there along the banks. One day Tommy and a friend drove up there on a weekday to do some work. When they pulled into the camp, they noticed what appeared to be two legs visible under a clump of leaves next to a tree about thirty yards away. Tommy put the car in park and both men watched as the legs swayed from side to side as if the "owner" was trying to get a look at their car. Suddenly, it stepped back from the tree into the sunlight. Now the men could see it was a tall, dark, humanoid figure. Tommy said it made eye contact, and as soon as it did, the thing bolted toward the lake. It ran like a deer, instantly at full speed.

Tommy jumped out of the car and tried to chase it, but it had already disappeared into a thicket of cypress and tupelo trees. He could hear splashing footsteps as whatever it was ran into the waters of Jeems Bayou.

Tommy described it as being quite tall, perhaps seven feet, and fairly lean with skin or hair that was shiny in the sun. He surmised it was shiny because it was wet. Neither Tommy nor his friend would admit it was a "Bigfoot" per se but were adamant they saw something that day they could not explain. It was disturbing, to say the least.

In 1999, Eric Holley was fishing near Jeems Bayou around dusk when he thought he heard someone walking through the woods. He looked up and saw a figure moving in the trees, but it wasn't a person. It appeared to be some kind of large, hair-covered animal.

"It was big; eight-foot tall probably," Holley told Ken Gerhard and I as we interviewed him in the Jefferson General Store one afternoon. "I've seen bears before, and I knew it wasn't a bear."

The creature never looked at Holley as it passed by. It simply moved further into the woods and eventually out of sight.

Holley was awestruck. He'd heard the legends of Bigfoot in East Texas but wasn't sure he believed. "Never in your wildest dreams do you think you're gonna see something like that," he told us. Now he has new perspective about what might be out there.

I have been in Jeems Bayou several times myself, and I find it to be one of the most eerie and unsettling places in all of East Texas—at least when the sun goes down. There's a certain quietness there that's both refreshing and spooky. I can't help but think of these stories every time I'm down there.

Jeems Bayou in the winter
(Note that the dark ground area is not solid ground—
it's water covered with moss and debris!)
(Photo by Lyle Blackburn)

Sightings like these are also prevalent on the eastern side of Caddo Lake in Louisiana, dating back many years. Several years ago I spoke to two witnesses—a brother and sister—who recounted a brief but harrowing incident they experienced as children around 1947. At the time they were staying at their family's camp house, which sat on the edge of Caddo Lake near Mooringsport. One evening after dark, as their parents visited with relatives, they were looking out the front window toward the lake when they saw a man-like thing peer inside. It had hair on its face and they could see hair on its arms as it raised a hand to the glass. The frightened siblings screamed and ran from the window.

After telling the adults what they'd seen, several of them hurried outside to investigate, but whatever had been there was already gone. They found no trace of tracks but estimated its height to be at least seven feet tall. The house sat on elevated piers and it would have been impossible for an average-sized man to be eye level with the window.

More recently in 2008, Faye Allen said she was headed to pick up some bagged pecans in a tractor when she noticed a large figure bent over one of the sacks. It appeared to be eating pecans. When she got within seventy feet, the thing stood up. Much to her surprise, it was a hairy, bipedal creature. She described it as being very tall, somewhat slender, and covered in solid black fur. Allen said she could not believe her eyes as the animal turned and looked directly at her. After a few moments it simply walked off into the woods.

A short time later, Ben DuPont—who lives one quarter mile from Caddo Lake—said he was awakened by a banging noise one night. When he went outside to investigate he saw a huge, hairy creature shaking a metal trailer where he kept several hogs. The hogs were making a frightened fuss as the beast tried to force its way in. As DuPont approached with a gun, the creature turned and looked at him. It appeared to be a female with breasts. The creature then made a huffing sound and took off bipedally across a field. When it reached the tree line, it howled before disappearing into the darkness.

It's interesting to note that Caddo Lake is close to the small town of Jefferson, Texas. Not only is Jefferson officially recognized as the "Bigfoot Capital of Texas," it is reputed to be one of the most haunted small towns in America. Sightings of ghostly figures have been reported in many of this old town's buildings and establishments, including plantation-type homes and hotels.

The most famous of Jefferson's ghostly tales is the one involving movie director Steven Spielberg, who came to Jefferson in the 1970s to film *Sugarland Express*. After a long day of shooting, he and his crew checked into the Excelsior House, a hotel said to be very haunted. Spielberg was assigned to the Gould Room in the east wing. According to the story, when he first walked into his room, he tossed his briefcase on a chair. The briefcase came flying right back at him! The incident was disturbing, but he finally managed to fall asleep. At around 2:00 a.m., however, the director was awakened by what appeared to be a small boy. The boy asked if he was ready for breakfast. At that point Spielberg shot out of bed, rounded up his weary crew, and made them leave.

"I swear my room was haunted," Spielberg told columnist John Anders of the *Dallas Morning News*. "I made everyone wake up, pack up, and get back in the cars at about two o'clock in the morning. We had to drive 20 miles to the nearest Holiday Inn, and everybody was hot at me. I am not normally superstitious."[177]

Coincidentally, Spielberg wrote the screenplay for his hit movie, *Poltergeist*, shortly thereafter.

Like the other anchor points of the Caddo Triangle, Caddo Lake and its bayous have a long association with regional filmmaking. It was used as the location for the swamp scenes in *Creature from Black Lake* (1976), the film inspired by the legends from Bayou Bodcau. *Creature from Black Lake* was not as monetarily successful as its influential predecessor, *The Legend of Boggy Creek*, although it still ranks today as one of the best Bigfoot-themed movies ever made. More recently, Caddo Lake was used as the film location for *Boggy Creek: The Legend is True*, released in 2010. While this movie has nothing to do with the original, it draws influence from *The Legend of Boggy Creek* for its title and, of course, *Creature from Black Lake* for its scenery. The low-budget indie, *Skookum: The Hunt for Bigfoot* (2014) also used Caddo Lake as the backdrop for many of its most effective scenes.[v]

The magnificence of Caddo Lake, from its scenic beauty to its spooky legends and film history, make this destination one

v Coincidentally, my late friend Tom Shirley, who explored much of Caddo Lake with me, had a small role in *Skookum: The Hunt For Bigfoot*.

of the most intriguing upon our journey. It is somewhat ironic that I didn't visit Caddo Lake until I was an adult. It's certainly much closer to my Texas home than Florida, yet Florida was the first place I was able to experience a swamp. Luckily, I can now feed my swampy fascination with a quick drive to Caddo or to the next swamp whose legend looms larger than any when it comes to creepy creatures who walk the shadowlands of great southern mysteries.

Boating to Devil's Elbow in Caddo Lake
(L to R: Charles Fason, Lyle Blackburn, Ken Gerhard, Tom Shirley)
(Photo by Taylor James Johnson)

Mercer Bayou / Boggy Creek

The third and final point of the Caddo Triangle terminates at the origin of the most infamous Southern Bigfoot legend ever. The name Mercer Bayou may not be as well-known as the associated tributary of Boggy Creek, yet Mercer Bayou's scenery and sightings are a huge part of the aforementioned cult classic film, *The Legend of Boggy Creek*. I've written extensively about the Boggy Creek area and its titular creature, the Fouke Monster, in several of my previous books, so I will attempt to spare repetition and focus specifically on the history of Mercer Bayou as it pertains to our sinister swamp exploration. As a part of the most famous Southern monster legend, it's a destination we cannot overlook.

For those who aren't familiar with the movie, *The Legend of Boggy Creek* was the directorial debut of the late Charles B. Pierce (*The Town That Dreaded Sundown*, *The Evictors*), who put aside a career in advertising to pursue filmmaking. Pierce was living in Texarkana, Arkansas, in 1971 and, like most residents in the area, was following sensational newspaper reports about a mysterious Bigfoot-like creature sighted in the nearby rural town of Fouke. Known locally as the "Fouke Monster," the creature had been seen by several prominent locals, and in one case, allegedly attacked a family at their home. The horrifying beast was said to be six or seven feet tall with ape-like features and long, shaggy hair, which often obscured its face. It was a backwoods nightmare come to life.

Pierce, wanting to capitalize on the media frenzy, borrowed some money, rented a camera, and set out to make a documentary about the beast. The film's concept eventually morphed from straight documentary to a hybrid horror movie/documentary that went on to reap amazing results once it secured distribution in theaters and drive-ins around the country.

The Legend of Boggy Creek is more or less a series of reenacted encounters with the Fouke Monster and does not follow a typical movie format consisting of rehearsed dialog. Pierce enlisted amateur actors and actual Fouke residents to recreate the alleged incidents using more improv and overdubs than rehearsed script. It was all tied together by a narrator who is recalling events from about 1963 to 1971. Much of the film's success relies on the authentic presence and accents of real Fouke residents and Texarkana locals, along with incredibly haunting scenery filmed around Days Creek and Mercer Bayou. The film's title is based on conjecture that the creature traveled up and down Boggy Creek— a ruddy tributary that snakes up and around Fouke—although in truth not many of the scenes were actually filmed on the creek itself. The name Boggy Creek sounds more forbidding, of course, so it was perfect for the movie title.

Geographically, Boggy Creek winds northwest from Fouke and feeds into Days Creek and eventually into the Sulphur River. Mercer Bayou originates just south of Days Creek with its main channel zigzagging through the Sulphur River Bottoms like a lazy snake. It widens in many areas to create a quintessential swamp, complete with cypress trees laden with Spanish moss. If one were to imagine a spooky swamp, Mercer Bayou would definitely fit the bill.

Mercer Bayou's significance to the Boggy Creek mystery, and the Caddo Triangle as a whole, can be traced back many years. Hunters and trappers who trekked into its expanse early on whispered of something strange living there. The Crabtree family, who plays a prominent role in *The Legend of Boggy Creek* movie and stories, had experiences close to their home, which backed up to Days Creek just a short distance from the wilds of Mercer Bayou. In 1964, Lynn Crabtree was squirrel hunting one evening on the back of their property when he sat down against a tree and dozed off. Lynn was awakened a short time later when he heard the sound of horses splashing into the waters of their lake. He then heard the bellowing of a dog from the same direction. With this, Lynn got up and headed toward the sound, thinking perhaps their dog might have been injured or gotten hung up in a fence. But as he approached, he realized the noise must have been coming from the *thing* that now stood in front of him. It was some kind of "hairy man or gorilla type beast with very long arms."[178] Lynn realized it had been the reason the horses fled into the safety of the lake.

The thing, which seemed agitated, stood still when it caught sight of Lynn. He could see it was seven or eight feet tall with reddish-brown hair about four inches long. Its face was obscured by hair with "only a dark brown nose showing, flat and close to his face." Thinking it must surely be a man, Lynn raised his gun in an attempt to frighten him off. But the strange "manimal" didn't react to the gun and now started walking toward the boy. Frightened, Lynn shouted a warning before firing off a round. He aimed for the head, but the beast seemed totally unaffected as it continued to advance. The Crabtree boy shot off two more rounds before finally fleeing in panic.

The encounter would have a significant effect on him and his family for the rest of their lives. Lynn never saw it again, but several of his relatives admitted they'd also seen such a beast while hunting and fishing in the bottoms around Mercer. They had never told their stories before, thinking that people would think they're crazy but were willing to tell once Lynn's story got out. They could not allow the boy to think he was alone in his strange experience. Lynn's father, J.E. "Smokey" Crabtree, essentially made it his life's work to find and prove the existence of the creature that had given his son nightmares. Though he was never able to prove it, Smokey documented many sightings that would have otherwise been lost. Up until his death in 2016, Smokey was an important figure in the Boggy Creek mystery.

Butch Hamilton claims to have seen a spooky, ape-like creature at the Mercer boat ramp in 1971. This was during the heyday of reports that first brought public attention to the Boggy Creek Monster case.[vi] I stood on a dirt road near the bayou while

---

vi Sightings in the 1960s and earlier – including those by the Crabtrees – were not publicized until 1971.

Hamilton told me of his haunting experience.

It was fall of '71 and Butch was going boating with his mother and father. When they pulled into Mercer's public boat ramp, he noticed a medium-sized camper parked at the north end of the circular parking area near the woods. The camper look well-used and had streams of rust running down its dirty, white exterior. A Suburban-type car was parked in front of it, but no occupants could be seen.

Butch's father made a U-turn and backed the boat trailer down to the water. When he came to a stop, Butch and his mother jumped out of their truck. He loved to explore the area around the ramp, so he wasted no time dragging his mother toward the trees to look for animal tracks or other interesting things.

Butch's father took to the task of preparing their boat. It was a ruddy green craft with a motor that did not always live up to its expectations. This time it must have needed more coaxing, since his father grabbed a toolbox from the back of their truck.

While his father worked on the boat, Butch and his mother collected pull-can tabs from the dirt and poked around in the leaves. He wouldn't mind if the old boat motor never started; he could have plenty of fun right there. Besides, the bayou got a little creepy at night. He knew his mother and father would not put him in danger, but still there was something about the hanging moss and groaning bullfrogs that could make a ten-year-old boy feel uneasy out on the dark water.

Butch and his mother continued to walk around the perimeter of the parking area. At one point he thought he could see movement inside the white camper, but so far no one had emerged. His mother was just about to go check on his father when something howled from the woods north of the camper. At first he thought it might be a bird, but after hearing it a second time, he could tell it was definitely an animal noise. It sounded like a coarse, moaning howl.

Butch's mother heard the sound, too, and tilted her head upward as if listening intently. She then attempted to call back by imitating the sound as closely as she could. Butch was impressed at how close she came. His mother was nearly full-blooded Native American and always took pride in her connection to animals and nature. This was the type of thing she really enjoyed.

After a few moments the animal made its strange cry again, this time ending the howl with something of a scream. Was it responding to his mother? She cupped her hand to her mouth and called back. The sound echoed into the woods, which were just beginning to fill with the late-afternoon shadows. This time the animal howled back immediately, sounding much closer.

As his mother made a third response, the door of the white camper opened. Butch saw one man, then two more emerge and step down onto the parking lot. They looked at him and his mother briefly, then turned toward the woods. One of them held a shotgun.

Butch and his mother watched with apprehension as the three men made their way around the camper to get a better look into the trees. As they rounded the corner, Butch could hear something approaching. It sounded like a man walking through the leaves. Butch felt a chill run up his back. What started out as exciting was starting to get very spooky.

The men said nothing, which must have made his mother even more nervous. She prompted him to head back toward the truck where his father was still tinkering with the boat, oblivious to what was happening at the other end of the drive. When Butch got halfway to the truck, he turned and looked back toward the woods. At that point he saw a hairy, reddish-brown creature walk into view. It stood perhaps seven to eight feet tall, but it hunched slightly as it stopped and looked at the men. It appeared to be studying them from the safety of the trees.

Butch bolted for the truck and jumped inside. His mother,

not having seen the creature, was walking toward the water where his father was working. Butch continued to observe the creature from the car. It slowly moved closer, stepping up onto an old log, but still keeping a safe distance from the men who remained by the camper. The man with the shotgun gripped it with both hands, but did not raise it.

Through the open window of the cab, Butch could hear his mother saying something to his father, but otherwise the whole scene was suspended in a strange, surreal silence. He watched for what seemed like several minutes as the creature held its wary position among the trees. The men, like Butch, merely observed in awe, as if they couldn't figure out what course of action to take. He glanced at his parents, who were still standing near the boat. His father seemed angry and was having a heated conversation with his mother.

Butch turned his attention back to the creature, which now stepped over the log. For a moment he wondered if it was going to run out and attack the men, but the thought was shattered when he heard the boat motor roar to life. At that point the creature turned and darted into the trees out of sight.

Butch backed away from the window and scrambled out of the cab. As he ran toward his mother, he prayed the boat motor would just sputter out and quit. He did not want to take a ride into the bayou that night. Whatever was living in those woods, he did not want to see again. He would not be the only one to have such a feeling.

A decade later, Harry Elrod said he was checking his trotline in the Mercer Bayou area known as "The Deadening," at around 10:00 p.m. when he saw something he can never get out of this mind. It was a clear night with a sliver of moonlight illuminating the black water. Elrod was in his boat with the motor off, kneeling in the front of craft so he could pull up the line to check each drop for fish. As he pulled on the line, he suddenly felt a "strong tug" on the far end. Thinking he had a really big fish, he hurried along with excitement. When he got to the point of resistance, he found he could not lift the line out of the water there. Thinking it was probably a snag, he was starting to cut the line when "a tall, hairy figure rose from the water with the line in its hand."[179]

Elrod immediately dropped the line and reeled back in horror. He then jumped into the shallow water and scrambled to the bank as fast as he could. From there he ran several miles through the woods until he came to a house near Blackman Ferry Road. He knocked on the door and pleaded with the owners to let him use the phone to call the Miller County Sheriff's Office. A deputy responded and subsequently investigated the area where he'd been working the trotline, but could find no trace of the creature. Elrod thought it was strange that he'd caught no fish over the last few days. Perhaps the creature, in its hunger, had been stealing them from the line.

One of the most dramatic encounters with the beast in Mercer Bayou was reported by a coon hunter. On a cold, moonlit night in the winter of 2000, he and several other men were coon hunting in an area of Mercer known as Thornton Wells. At some point, one of the hunter's dogs treed a raccoon deep in the swamp. He followed his dog's lead and separated from the other men. After locating the coon and collecting his dog, the hunter started back across the swamp to rejoin the group when he heard something "walking in the flooded timber." Thinking it was one of his fellow hunters, the man called out.

"To my dismay no one answered—instead all I heard was a deep throated gurgling growl and [smelled] the awfullest [sic] putrid smell," he explained. "I also heard a whining kind of a whistling sound."[180]

The dogs began whimpering and cowering behind the coon hunter's legs, which struck him as very unusual for such experienced hounds. The hunter was puzzled, but unconcerned, so he gathered his dogs and started back across the swamp.

"After a few minutes I heard this sound of someone or something walking in the water again," he continued. "So I stopped and turned around and standing right behind me was a creature of immense size." The thing was hulking and huge, covered in dark, rusty-brown hair that was wet and matted. The skin on its face and hands was "gray and leathery," and while its overall characteristics were ape-like, its face was "like that of a person." It stood upright on two legs in the shallow water as it flashed its teeth at the awestruck hunter. His recollection is chilling:

> *I don't ever remember being that scared. He made a hissing sound and reached down and took his hand and started scooping water and throwing it up at me and making a deep throaty noise. My dogs started chomping at the leash and growling trying to get at it, having regained their bravery. I grabbed the leash and tore out across that swamp so scared that, for a while, I went in the wrong direction. I got to a big cypress knee and caught my breath. I could hear the thing behind me, it sounded like it was about 100 yards or so back. It followed me for a ways, then after a while I could hear it across the bayou making a moaning sound and moving away slowly.*
>
> *I got my breath and my compass and my bearings and started back to the truck. When I got there I didn't say a word to my friends about what I saw and heard for fear they would laugh. Needless to say I never returned to Thornton Wells nor do I plan to. For a long time I kept this to myself. I even had nightmares about it.*[181]

I've been to Mercer Bayou myself many times, tromping through its flooded forestry and camping on its banks. One night in June 2014, I was canoeing up the bayou channel around midnight with my late friend, Tom Shirley, when we heard a distinctive howl about one hundred yards away. We immediately stopped paddling and listened closely. About forty-five seconds later, the animal howled again. At first I thought it could have been a very unusual coyote, but after hearing it a second time I knew it wasn't. Tom, who was a very experienced outdoorsman and trapper, agreed. Whatever this was, it was not a typical Arkansas animal.

A minute later, the thing made the vocalization again. It began as a throaty moan and ended with a high, howling scream that echoed eerily across the moonlit swamp. This time we were certain it was not a coyote, cougar, fox, bear, or anything else we could easily identify. The back of my neck tingled. The experience was both exciting and chilling.

Tom and I continued to listen, but the animal did not howl again. We were exhilarated, thinking perhaps we'd heard the legendary Fouke Monster, yet disappointed when it went silent. We'd gone far enough up the bayou from our camp at Thornton Wells, so we decided to turn around and head back.

We discussed the characteristics of the howl as we paddled through the carpet of duckweed that choked the channel during the warm seasons. It made it difficult to get the canoe through at times. We passed some alligators whose eyes peered at us just above the surface of the water. There were plenty of them in Mercer Bayou, especially around Thornton Wells.

When we arrived at the campsite location, we pulled the canoe out of the water and headed up a hill where our tent was pitched. It was approximately forty yards from the water behind a stand of trees that lined the channel. About the time we got to our tent, we heard the howl again—this time originating just across the channel where we had just been! Tom scrambled to turn on his audio recording device as I grabbed the nearest flashlight. A mere thirty to forty-five seconds later the animal howled a second time. I was sure it was standing somewhere at the bottom of the hill, just across the channel. Without thinking, I turned on the flashlight and ran pell-mell through the trees down the hill trying to focus the beam on the place where I thought the thing might be standing. When I got to the edge of the water, I scanned the trees on the other side, hoping I could get a glimpse of it. I thought I heard something running but couldn't quite tell. As I stood there pumped with adrenaline, the thing howled yet again. This time, however, it was further away in the woods. The animal had moved away as swiftly as it had come.

A band of coyotes began yipping nervously in response to the howl, but neither Tom nor I heard it again. If it was the infamous Boggy Creek Monster, it was not going to reveal itself to us that night.

Something did reveal itself to Dustin Clark, however, and very recently. On the night of December 7, 2019, Clark and several friends were scouting a wooded area at the north end of Mercer Bayou when Clark decided to walk ahead by himself. The moon was bright and provided enough ambient light to see into the woods without having to turn on the intrusive beam of his headlamp. After he was away from the group, Clark knelt down and scanned the dark road ahead looking for any signs of nocturnal wildlife. He saw something move. It was the silhouette of a large figure walking between two trees to his left.

"What caught my eye was actually the moonlight; it was glaring off the hair on the back of the head, the shoulder, and the back of the arm as it was moving left to right," Clark explained in a video he shared with me. "When I looked over, I could see the shape go across."

The shape disappeared behind some trees as Clark grappled with the possibilities. "I was in disbelief, excited, and my adrenaline was pumping," he said.

Clark reacted quickly, calling to his friend Steven, who

had a pair of night vision binoculars. Steven hurried to where Clark was standing, and they began scanning the trees with the binoculars, hoping to catch another glimpse of the figure. They watched for several minutes, but nothing moved.

"I'd almost given up, when I looked over on the same side of the road—down in this gully—and I saw more movement," Clark continued. "It went between some trees."

Mercer Bayou (near Thornton Wells) south of Fouke, Arkansas (Photo by Lyle Blackburn)

He raised the binoculars again and began scanning the area around the trees. After some work to focus them, Clark finally locked onto the figure again. In the green-white hue of the night vision, Clark could see part of its head, face, and shoulders as it peered around the trunk of a tree and looked at him with white eyeshine. He was shocked; so shocked he momentarily pulled the binoculars away from his eyes. When both he and Steven looked again, the thing was no longer visible.

After some discussion, they decided to advance slowly toward the trees. When they got there, however, whatever Clark had seen was gone. It had apparently slipped away into the dark woods, leaving Clark with only the memory of a fleeting encounter—one that he will never forget.

The long history of these strange sightings in and around Mercer Bayou ties closely to the events made famous in *The Legend of Boggy Creek* movie and to the ongoing case of its ostensible monster. Though Mercer is not as famous as the related tributary, Boggy Creek, these waterways and their connection to one of the most enduring American monster mysteries of all time provide a solid anchor for the furthest reaches of the swampy, Caddo Triangle.

10

MORE MENACING MIRE

So far we've explored some of the most notable swamps and bayous across the North American landscape where strange things have been reported. Yet there are countless more dotting the continent (not to mention well beyond) where mysteries beckon like flickering lanterns in the misty darkness. Some of these are undoubtedly smaller and less well-known outside their own region, however, you will find they are undeniably worthy of a mention as we wind down our sinister study.

Hannah's Hanged Men

A rather notorious swamp-ghost story creeps from the shaded bogs of a place called Hannah's Creek Swamp in North Carolina. This notorious patch of coastal swampland is located at the north end of the densely thicketed Uwharrie National Forest, where ghostly tales and sightings of hairy, man-like creatures have existed for decades. Visitors to the realm of Hannah's Creek have reported hearing eerie noises like the creaking of ropes and the disembodied voices of men begging for their lives to be spared. The area was once the scene of the Civil War's final campaign conducted by the Union army against the Confederate army in the Western Theater, and its famous ghostly tale arises from this very conflict.

As the story goes, in 1865, the Union soldiers were marching through North Carolina as they made their way south. They were authorized to plunder homes and shake down individuals along the way, provided they left enough food and supplies for families to survive and did not cause harm to unarmed civilians.

Most soldiers adhered to these orders, however, one particular group of soldiers led by Colonel David Fanning did not. Fanning's platoon thought nothing of terrorizing civilians as they pillaged and plundered their way southward. Oftentimes after plundering a home, they left it in a burning blaze, which earned the rogue group a nasty reputation.

At Smithfield, Fanning's tactless men finally made a grave mistake when they plundered the home of Confederate Colonel John Saunders,[vii] killing both him and his wife in the process. Word eventually got around to their son, John Saunders Jr., who was also a colonel in the Confederate army. Col. Saunders Jr. was so enraged he vowed revenge on each man who had participated in the heinous act.

For weeks, Saunders scoured the land looking for the offenders. Finally, he got word they were encamped on a small island deep in the swamp of Hannah's Creek. The colonel quickly rounded up a small group of Confederate soldiers and led them to a town at the edge of the swamp. Once there, Saunders arranged for him and his men to borrow civilian clothes and a canoe from the townsfolk so they could approach the encampment without arousing suspicions. The next afternoon, the Confederates discretely rowed their way to the island, where they took Fanning and his men by surprise. When Saunders' men searched their gear, they found a small gold crucifix that had belonged to Saunders's mother. Saunders was so angry he held Fanning at gunpoint while he ordered his men to systematically hang each of the Union offenders by their neck from a crooked tree that grew on the island.

After they had executed each of the Union soldiers, Saunders transported Fanning back to his parents' plundered home in Smithfield and strung him up by the neck from a tree that over-

---

vii I was not able to confirm that a Confederate colonel by the name of John Saunders actually served in the Civil War. There was, however, a violent loyalist named Colonel David Fanning in the Carolinas area during the Revolutionary War. Such is the nature of legends where facts and names may become mixed up.

looked the family cemetery. It was crude justice, but justice that Saunders felt was undeniably due.

There were undoubtedly many cruelties perpetrated during the tragic War between the States, and perhaps, if this story is to be believed, some of them left a trace behind. Visitors to the modern-day location of Hannah's Creek Swamp have since claimed to experience extreme "cold spots" in the hot, humid environment, along with "unexplained feelings of dread."[182] These have often been accompanied by a sound that seems like ropes creaking. Even more disturbing, some people have reported hearing voices that are apparently pleading for their lives. Are these the lingering voices of Colonel Fanning's marauders? Only the secretive swamp knows for sure.

Chatawa Monsters

While investigating reports of unexplained phenomena, I often come across eyewitnesses whose stories stick with me long after the conversation. These chilling accounts would seem as though they've been plucked from the script of a masterful horror film, if not for the credibility of the witnesses themselves.

I recently came across one such witness while delving into the Chatawa Swamp in southwest Mississippi. The swamp—which is a rugged, forested floodplain along the Tangipahoa River— has long been rumored to harbor everything from black panthers to two-headed serpents to wild monkeys (which was proven!), while reports of a hairy creature known as the "Chatawa Monster" are the most prevalent. The witness in this case, Jacquelyn Cooper, told me she and her ex-husband came across just such a creature in 1997. That night they were enjoying the evening in a remote part of their vast property near Chatawa Swamp. They were sitting in the back of their truck listening to music when a major thunderstorm rolled in. Rather than drive in it, the couple decided to wait it out. After the storm subsided, they started to leave but found the truck battery had died because of the radio and lights. Fearing more storms would come during the night, they decided to walk to the nearby town.

"As we walked, the lightening was still flashing in the sky so it illuminated the path along with what little moon peeked through the clouds," Jacquelyn recalled. They did not have a flashlight, but her husband had a .22 pistol, so they felt safe enough—that is until they noticed the silhouette of huge, man-like figure standing about forty yards ahead. At first they assumed it was a person, but its size, shape, and broad shoulders did not look quite human. And the more Jacquelyn looked, the more she began to realize it was more "thing" than man.

"My ex-husband yelled it was private property and they needed to identify themselves," she explained. There was no response, so he fired the pistol into the air. "All of a sudden the most horrible growl and scream came from whatever it was. I was scared out of my mind."

Panicked, Jacquelyn's husband fired shots toward the thing until the clip ran out. Whether from the noise or being struck by a bullet, the thing then began to thrash around "breaking limbs and yelling." At that point the couple ran, fleeing right through the trees since the thing was still blocking their path.

"I just remember running, and my ex running behind me, and those screams echoing through the woods," Jacquelyn said.

They ran nearly four miles to the town, never looking back. The next day, when they returned to retrieve the truck, they stopped at the location where the thing had been standing. There they found several huge, man-like tracks that didn't look like they'd been made by a human or even a bear.

"I will never doubt anything else that might be out there," Jacquelyn confessed. "And I will never be able to forget that night nor those screams."

The Chatawa Monster was nothing new. Reports of an alleged swamp creature date back many years. Some of the oldest ones, told by old-timers in the area, describe it as being more serpent-like with two heads. This description seemed to transform over the years to that of a more Bigfoot-like thing as actual witnesses began to describe their encounters. Local resident Phillip O'Brien said he'd heard tails of a strange animal that had been seen by a train engineer in the early 1960s. Wanda Moyer was also familiar with the legend, having heard it from friends and family all her life. She told me she and ten friends had even gone looking for the thing one night around 1976. Late that evening they'd assembled in town and were debating what to do for fun. When someone suggested they go down to the Chatawa bottoms and look for the creature, they decided to do just that.

"We were there about an hour maybe when we heard a noise like nothing I've ever heard before," Moyer told me. "Something was coming through the woods really fast, and it was trampling down huge bushes and small trees."

As the unseen thing came toward them, they could hear its heavy footsteps. It was breathing loudly and occasionally let out a bloodcurdling scream. It was enough to spook the entire group.

"It kept getting closer, and the hair stood up on the back of my neck," she admitted. "Everyone ran for their cars and trucks so fast. If I had not been there myself I would not have believed it."

Though they didn't get a clear sighting of the noisemaker, incidents like these continued to bolster the idea that something monstrous was inhabiting the forbidding maze of Chatawa Swamp. So far there had not been any alleged physical evidence, but that would change in 1980.

In late fall of that year, longtime Chatawa resident, Jack Hays, was walking the creek behind Sunshine Mountain Church and Children's Home when he came upon some rather unusual footprints in the sandy soil.[183] They resembled a bare human foot, yet were much larger than an average man's foot, measuring over fourteen inches long and five inches wide. The depth suggested that whatever had made them was heavy.

Hays had been losing chickens lately from his chicken coop. Not one at a time, but ten or more at a time. He could not figure out what kind of animal was responsible or how it had gotten in.

"I've never heard of any animal that kills more than he eats," Hays remarked to a reporter at the time. He'd made a call to the newspaper—after much prodding from his family—but requested they didn't print anything until after an open house he had planned for the Sunshine Mountain Children's Home. He knew this whole thing sounded crazy, but could not deny something strange may be going on.

About the time Jack's chickens started disappearing, his nephew, Ralph Hays, Jr., had seen similar tracks on the creek. He was so impressed they got some plaster and cast one of the prints. Jack could see what looked like a scar on the foot, which struck him as very odd.

"Awhile back I was down at the well and I met an 83-year-old man," Hays said. "He said a few years back, he told one of his children to go cut some wood. He took a double-bitted axe and went out and chopped some wood, and he left the axe sticking in a log. Well, later that night they heard a scream, and when they went out they found blood around that axe, and a blood trail leading off in the woods."

Hays didn't think much about it until he saw the strange footprint cast. Coincidentally, it had a scar that could have been made by an axe. In looking at the newsprint photo, the footprint seems a bit too "perfect," but then again the sandy soil along the creek bank would be ideal for capturing impressions. Hays did not want to speculate as to whether the tracks had been made by the infamous Chatawa Swamp Monster or whether such a creature was responsible for stealing his chickens, but he wasn't ruling it out.

The Chatawa Swamp is a foreboding place that meanders through the Mississippi mud like a lazy viper. In the late evening, the forested canopy and dark, shadowed waters give off an eerie vibe which is ominous in its stunning stillness. Quiet naturally, the tales of intrigue that surround it seem ever present. Rumors that a circus train crashed there in the 1930s have persisted among the locals. The crash supposedly let loose a pair of black panthers, which had been seen off and on for years. A woman who requested her name be kept off the record told reporter Ernest Herndon she "had personally observed a black panther which had been shot and killed by a railroad man."[184]

Perhaps even more strange, a rumor surfaced in 1998 that a nun at the St. Mary of the Pines convent in Chatawa had been attacked by a monkey! A swamp monkey? When this came across the desk of Ernest Herndon, he immediately dropped what he was doing and set out to get the scoop. Perhaps this was related to the old rumor of the circus train, he thought. Could a family of monkeys have survived all those years in the bottoms?

Herndon first located a woman by the name of Joyce Clement who said she saw a monkey cross the road in Chatawa in the winter of 1996.

"I was heading from the railroad track on to St. Mary of the Pines, and this monkey swung out of a tree and landed in the road and stood up," Clement said. "When I put on my brakes, I guess he heard the motor and took off running."

She was absolutely sure it was a monkey and not anything else. "There is a monkey," she confirmed. "It was a monkey with a long tail." She estimated it was about two and half feet tall when it stood up on its hind legs.

When Clement told one of the sisters at the convent, the

nun casually mentioned that she'd been bitten twice by monkeys. When Herndon contacted the nun for her story, she unfortunately dispelled the rumor that she had been attacked by the Chatawa Monkey. Her attack had occurred many years earlier. When she was a teenager she'd been bitten by someone's pet monkey.

Enterprise-Journal Sunday, Oct. 12, 1980

Enterprise-Journal Outdoors

Leather Britches

Monster tales from Chatawa

By ERNEST HERNDON
Enterprise-Journal Staff Writer

At last a clear, concise description of the Chatawa Monster has emerged from those black boggy woods in southern Pike County.

Vague rumors of the monster have circulated throughout the area for years, and the beast has been described alternately as a Bigfoot, an ape, a bear, a panther, or any combination thereof.

Now two conflicting reports emerge: one, an age-old description drawn from the tales of Chatawa grandfathers; the other, a real-life

McComb barber Obie Milton once told of a frightening encounter he had not too many years ago in the woods around Chatawa.

Milton was at Nunnery's Men's Store, that gathering place of yarn-spinners, when he related his experience.

He said he was squirrel hunting alone and seeing a squirrel he shot it from the tree. On approaching the dead squirrel, however, he came upon a "tall, hairy fellow" who stood menacingly over the squirrel, as if to say, "This is mine."

"I let him have it," Milton said with a nervous laugh.

And he beat a quick retreat.

One of the many news articles discussing the Chatawa Monster (Enterprise-Journal – October 12, 1980)

Despite the fail with the nun-attack story, it was strange enough that a monkey was roaming the Chatawa Swamp, given its propensity for weird stories. At least in this case there was little doubt that the witness did indeed see some type of monkey. When asked if they believed there were any monkeys in Chatawa, Pike

County wildlife conservation officers said they'd received no such reports. If monkeys had been living in the swamp since the circus train wreck, then surely someone would have spotted them before 1996.

Unfortunately the story of the Chatawa Monkey went cold from there. There have been no other sightings or explanation as to the origin of the primate. The best we can do, for now, is add the Chatawa Monkey to the mysterious menagerie lurking in this strange and fertile ground known as the Chatawa Swamp.

Bear Creek Bog

If we take a drive eastward from Chatawa up to the very heart of Alabama, we'll find ourselves in another of the Deep South's most notorious bottomlands: Bear Creek Swamp. This murky bog—located in Autauga County just west of the capital city of Montgomery—is literally simmering with spookiness from ghosts to phantom cars to creepy dolls. Bear Creek Swamp is so notorious, in fact, it is cited as one of the top seven most terrifying places in Alabama![185]

Some of the oldest tales speak of ghosts who roam the swamp at witching hour. These are said to be spirits of Native Americans who once lived in the region, or perhaps settlers or Civil War soldiers who perished in its foreboding murkiness. The swamp was the site of a Creek Indian village, which remained there until 1814. Many of its occupants were veterans of the Creek War, a regional battle between opposing Creek factions. Many souls did indeed perish in the vicinity of Bear Creek, and surely blood has been spilled in its black waters.

A woman from Prattville, Alabama, told my fellow researcher Alex Bobulinski she had visited Bear Creek several times and on one occasion saw a "figure which appeared to be wearing the confederate civil war uniform with a musket."

Over the years, people have also reported sightings of strange lights, "fire balls," and even a phantom car that speeds by, only to disappear a short distance later. According to paranormal investigator Shawn Sellers, he and his team had set up cameras and were walking along one of the swamp roads when:

> *Suddenly, we saw two cars' headlights coming from opposite directions. As we backed off as far as we could to the side of the road, one of the cars raced past us suddenly going far faster than it should on such a road. We were afraid that there would be a collision. As we looked towards the other car, it slowly went past us in the opposite direction. To our amazement there was no collision or even a beeped horn. There was no place for the speeding car to go except into the swamp. We raced back to the well where we had our camera facing the road. We rewound the tape to see where the other car went and found no sign of the speeding car, only the slow car from the other direction.*[186]

In November 2016 Alex Bobulinski was investigating Bear Creek Swamp himself when he *did* catch something on camera. "I was getting my camera set up on the back of my car," Alex explained, when: "All of a sudden in the rearview mirror I see this light show up and it got bigger and bigger. Then all of a sudden it gets smaller and smaller and fades out."[187] Alex believes he caught what people refer to as the "phantom car" on video. Perhaps this was some lingering "image" of a vehicle and its driver who had an unfortunate accident while driving through swamp.

This theory could also apply to one of the more disturbing legends that has come out of Bear Creek—that of the Ghostly Mother. According to some, the ghost of a grieving mother roams the dense woods looking for her lost child. Her eerie, wailing voice cries out in the darkness, echoing the endless sorrow she feels. If anyone is brave enough to utter the phrase "we have your baby" three times, she will emerge from the shadows and attack. This may sound like an ubiquitous urban legend, but not according to one story.

According to the main witness, he and several friends drove out to Bear Creek Swamp late one night to hangout and drink. When they got there, they parked the car on a deserted road and got out. The driver pulled the key from the ignition and placed it on top of the car.

During the course of the evening, one of the group decided to call out "we have your baby." He said it three times, just as the legend demanded. Nothing happened at first, but a few seconds later they "heard a rustling sound in the bushes like something slowly rolling towards them."[188] Spooked, the guys tried to get back in the car, but found the doors were inexplicably locked. The driver quickly grabbed the key and inserted it in the lock, but still the car door would not open. In the commotion one of the group began to scream in pain. His leg had been gashed open and blood was pouring out.

After several intense moments, the car doors suddenly unlocked and the men leapt inside and sped back to Highway 14. As they entered the highway, the guy whose leg was cut realized the pain was gone and the blood was no longer visible. "There was absolutely nothing wrong with his leg, not a scratch, despite numerous people seeing blood everywhere," concluded the report. Whatever happened that night remains a mystery.

If that's not enough to qualify Bear Creek as a sinister swamp, then perhaps the next incident will. According to author Faith Serafin in her book *Haunted Montgomery Alabama*, a young couple decided to take an afternoon hike through the wilds of Bear Creek Swamp. As they were hiking through a dense, swampy area near the creek, "they saw what appeared to be a scantily clad and unusual woman crouching at the bank."[189] She looked to be in distress, so the couple approached her, hoping they could help. As they got closer, they could see she was very gaunt with unusually pale skin and thin, matted white hair. Her clothes were "torn and mangled," revealing a thin, skeletal form.

When the man reached for the woman's shoulder, she turned with "an awkward jerk" and glared with "fierce yellow eyes." She had a sunken, skeletal face which startled the couple. Before they could say anything, the woman stood up and let out a loud, frightening shriek as she "flailed her arms about in panic." She then turned and ran swiftly into the dense trees. The couple ran after her, but she outpaced them and disappeared into the shadowy brush. They continued to search for some time, thinking she may have collapsed somewhere, but never found her.

The couple was so disturbed by the encounter they decided to report it to the local sheriff's office. "It is unclear if the local authorities followed up on the event, but neither of these individuals would dare step foot in the Bear Creek Swamp again." And who could blame them?

In 2014, the spooky reputation of Bear Creek made national news when authorities removed twenty-one "creepy dolls" from the swamp. According to an article in *USA Today*, Chief Deputy Joe Sedinger first noticed the dolls while driving on a dirt road through the swamp between Prattville and Autaugaville.[190] They appeared to be some kind of antique dolls with pale faces and tattered clothing. They were visible from the road because they were impaled atop bamboo stakes.

Sedinger didn't think too much about it as he continued on to his destination, although given the reputation of the swamp, it did seem rather creepy. A few days later, however, "social media blew up about the dolls, and the office got wind of the concerns." Residents in the area were naturally concerned about the purpose of the dolls, whether it be to simply scare people or whether it was an indication of something sinister going on. At this point, deputies felt they should investigate the site where the dolls had been placed.

On Tuesday, November 25, deputies brought canoes to the location and paddled around for thirty minutes inspecting the area and the dolls themselves. They didn't find any signs of occult activity or anything of that nature but felt it might be best to remove the dolls anyway. "I admit it looked kind of creepy," Sedinger said. "You could see them from the road. We figured it was best to get them up."

Upon examination, they found that the majority of the dolls were made of porcelain and appeared to be antique. Many had the faces and hair covered in what looked like white spray paint.

The land where the dolls were placed is owned by a timber company who did not respond to inquiries by the police. Neither the owner of the dolls nor the reason they were placed there has never been discovered. Like so many swamp mysteries, visible or immaterial, explanations are hard to come by.

Creepy Congaree

In the summer of 2018, Cindy and I visited one of the South's most majestic forested bottomlands, the Congaree National Park. The park is located near Columbia, South Carolina, and contains the largest contiguous expanse of old-growth bottomland hardwood forest in the United States. To describe it only as majestic is perhaps inadequate, as the region offers a habitat of amazing biodiversity from tracts of grand-canopied trees to breathtaking vistas to shadowed bogs where a sense of mystery permeates the air.

The swampy portions of the Congaree are fed by the waters of the Congaree and Wateree rivers, which nourish it with frequent influx. The park does not have standing water at all times, but the rivers do flood it up to ten times a year.[191] As expected, the environment here is filled with a variety of coastal floodplain flora and numerous animals and insect species.

For the exploration, Cindy and I met up with our good friend Mike Richburg. Mike is a native of South Carolina and is very familiar with the land and lore of the state. Mike and I first became friends when I learned of a sighting he had years ago in the area of the Congaree known as Devil's Orchard Swamp. He was hunting that morning when a tall, muscular, ape-like creature walked into a clearing forty feet away. It lingered a moment and sniffed the air before it walked off. The encounter left Mike in shock, although at the same time infused him with a keen interest in the phenomenon of unexplained creatures, which he shares with Cindy and me. The Congaree was the perfect backdrop to discuss our mutual interests and explore some of the South's most interesting swamp terrain.

We entered the park in the late afternoon and began our hike down a wooden boardwalk that hovers just above the soggy soil of the Congaree floor. As we creaked along the wooden walkway, the first thing I noticed was the incredibly high trees, which loomed above us like thin giants. Cindy shielded the afternoon sun from her eyes to gaze upward at the impressive canopy. Mike pointed out the old-growth forest here contains the largest concentration of what's known as "champion trees." These are the largest recorded living specimens of each tree variety found in the continental United States. The Congaree boasts fifteen species, including a 167-foot loblolly pine, a 157-foot sweetgum, and a 154-foot cherrybark oak.[192] The mixture of these giants among the bald cypress and water tupelo raised the swampy vibe to a new level of grandeur.

After exploring the boardwalk—which loops through the bottoms for more than two miles—we headed off on a muddy trail that led to one of the many creeks veining the area. Areas of thick foliage interspersed with pockets of standing water made it a challenge to navigate at times. We eventually skidded down an embankment and found ourselves in a secluded sanctuary that resembled a movie set with its picturesque layout. We marveled at the subtle beauty while breathing in the air of mystery, which seemed as palpable as the ghostly moss on the trees.

The Congaree National Park represents the best of what national parks have to offer, yet like all swampy places, it conceals a lesser-known, spooky side. One of the most prominent of the Congaree's dark tales is that of the "Swamp Lady." According to legend, a "well-dressed woman has been reportedly seen walking down a dark highway in the middle of the extremely dense Congaree swampland near Columbia."[193] In one case, a couple claimed they were driving toward Columbia when they saw a woman on the side of the road. They figured she was in trouble, so they stopped to offer a ride. The woman muttered a Columbia street address and got into the backseat. As they drove away, the wife asked the woman a question, but got no reply. When she turned and looked in the backseat, she was shocked to find the woman had "vanished into thin air, leaving behind an eerie vapor mist in her seat."

The wife was so unnerved, the husband had to take her to the hospital emergency room once they reached Columbia. He then drove to the house address on Pickens Street that the ghostly woman had given. An older lady answered the door, and judging by the pale look of the husband, guessed why he was there. She told him he was just one of many people who had come knocking on her door after an encounter with a vanishing woman. The "woman," she said, was actually the specter of her dead sister. She had been killed in an auto accident while driving through the swamp years ago. Since then she's roamed its byways after dark, summoning rides home that she never completes.

Visitors to the shadowed banks of Congaree Creek at Old

State Road claim to have heard the sound of men marching or have caught glimpses of phantom soldiers with their lanterns swinging in the darkness.[194] Not surprisingly, this was the site of a Civil War conflict known as the Battle of Congaree Creek. While marching through South Carolina in 1865, General Sherman's men killed nearly 1,500 Confederate soldiers who made a stand along the creek. The ground here is soaked with the blood of this tragedy, which some say anchors the spirits to the site.

Like most swamps we've explored, the Congaree is also rumored to harbor unusual creatures. During our visit, Mike told us of two instances in which a witness claimed to have seen a large, upright, hair-covered creature run across nearby roads. They were brief sightings, but enough to suggest the Congaree may be hiding a Southern Bigfoot or two. South Carolina might not rank high on the list of states where Bigfoot is thought to live (perhaps in favor of Lizard Man tales), but it does have a history of such sightings.

The author with Mike Richburg in the Congaree (Photo by Cindy Lee)

According to an 1889 edition of the *Clarksville Advertiser*, a Native hunting party was camped east of the Tugalo River (now called Tugaloo) along the South Carolina/Georgia border when a tall "monster animal" covered in hair and walking upright like a man tried to steal a deer carcass from their camp. Although one of the men could have shot it with his bow, he was too frightened to try.[195]

In 1938, locals in the town of Rock Hill, South Carolina, were said to be living in terror after a bipedal, hair-covered creature attacked a man and killed two dogs. According to *The Daily Gleaner* newspaper: "Constable Carl Hovis reported he saw the shambling beast in a dark back alley and shot at it twice but failed to bring it down."[196]

In recent times, a soldier from Fort Jackson was on a training mission in the Congaree (before it was a national park) when he had an extremely frightening experience. It was autumn 1964 and he was sent into the woods by himself as part of an escape and evasion exercise. At around 7:00 p.m., just after dark, he was walking along a dirt fire lane road when he heard something coming toward him in the dark. It was a moonless night, and visibility was very poor, but he could tell it was walking on two legs by the sound. Thinking it must be a person, the soldier stood and waited. When the footsteps got close, he asked "Who goes there?"[197]

"It went about fifty to seventy-five feet away and just stood there," he explained. "Then I heard what sounded like someone talking backwards in a sort of growl as I was standing there confused about what was going on."

After a tense minute, whatever it was started walking toward him again. This time the soldier knelt down on one knee and kept very still. When the figure came out of the trees, the soldier stood up and said "I got you! But it wasn't a person.

"That's when all hell brook loose," he explained. "It took off running, crashing through the brush like a train."

The incident was so frightening, the soldier began running down the fire lane in the dark. He ran a good distance before he finally stopped and listened. He hoped the thing wasn't coming after him. He stood there, alone in the dark, listening for any movement or breathing. The black moon provided no comfort. He was an experienced hunter and a confident soldier, but this was utterly terrifying.

After a few moments, he was satisfied the thing hadn't followed him, so he continued running in the opposite direction. Finally, he came upon a sergeant who was waiting in a truck at the extraction point.

"I never wanted to see a person so badly before," he admitted. Whatever lurked in the darkness of the Congaree, he did not want to encounter ever again.

The woods and waters of the Congaree seemed peaceful enough that day as Cindy, Mike, and I continued our hike through its vast reaches. The location did not make any of us apprehensive, but being in the thick, swampy terrain—which spread for miles and miles—I couldn't help but imagine what might be out there, waiting patiently for the shadows of darkness to come.

The Congaree does not have an abundance of paranormal reports, but perhaps that says something significant about the subject. The fact not all swamps have the same level of reports or distribution of phenomena—cryptids, ghosts, etc.—lends credibility to the incidents. In other words, if no one saw anything strange, then no one reported it. The incidents aren't simply manufactured. Our proclivity to find unusual things in these environments is certainly inherent, but not so much it clouds our every sense of reason. In the recesses of these swamp shadows, a very real phenomenon may indeed lurk. As we hiked on, it was the possibility of these mysteries we sought, hoping that someday one of them would pluck us from the daylight of our reality into the nighttime mists of the unexplained.

CONCLUSION

We've examined many strange tales during our soggy exploration. Some of these are obviously rooted in superstition and legend, while others are more tangible and hard to explain. Do monsters, ghosts, witches, and spook lights truly exist in these pockets of primordial earth? No one can say for sure. But if things like these are real, then perhaps a swamp is the most logical place for them to exist. These are often the most undeveloped areas of our landscape, where few people go and even fewer are likely to venture too far into its expanse. The rugged terrain and thick shadows afford a domain in which fringe creatures, spirits, and other bizarre phenomena could thrive in our modern times.

It's certainly possible some of the incidents can be explained by natural phenomena such as swamp gas (a mixture of methane, hydrogen sulfide, and carbon dioxide produced by the anaerobic digestion and fermentation of plant or animal matter) or mistaken identity (such as a bear for a Bigfoot) or even a trick of light and shadow within a spooky environment, but this doesn't seem sufficient to explain them all. The number of stories and consistency of their details begs us to consider stranger possibilities, even if only for a portion of the tales.

And while swamps can certainly be sinister, I must remind you they should not be dreaded or shunned. These important lands should be respected and relished for their role in our environment. Each facet of the wetland lifecycle, from flooding to flourishing, is a necessary part of our delicate ecology and a reminder that we are part of a complex system of existence; one we are still striving to understand.

That being said, the swamp will forever hold sway over our primal fears, making each chilling tale a bit more spooky and each legend a bit more gripping by virtue of its ominous backdrop of ghostly moss and crooked trees. It's a feeling that is surely interwoven into the very fabric of our psyche. Perhaps it's a remnant of our innate instinct for survival that has allowed us to endure in a world full of danger and unknowns. Or perhaps it stems from the very nature of swamps since they ultimately represent a sort of bubbling cauldron of life where our primeval past is still alive and strange things can—and do—exist. Whatever the case, the swamp will always represent a dark side of nature where black waters hold ancient secrets and twisted landscapes conceal mysteries and perils that are as valid today as they were ages ago.

So the next time you drive by a lonely grove of cypress trees rising from a pocket of dark, brackish water, be sure to look closely at the shadows within. You never know when *you* might see some strange, unexplainable thing creeping from the depths of a sinister swamp.

ACKNOWLEDGEMENTS

Special thanks to the following colleagues, friends, and family members who assisted with this book. Without them, it would not have been possible.

David Bakara, Alex "Bigfoot Bob" Bobulinski, Ashlen Brown, Ashley Cheree, Loren Coleman, Adam Davies, Danny Dupont, Charles and Michelle Fason, Ken Gerhard, John Gerard, Linda Godfrey, Jerry Hestand, Dana Holyfield, Richard Knox, Marc Lane, Cindy Lee, Dave McCullough, Matt Moneymaker and the BFRO, Wanda Moyer, Daniel Perez, Nick Redfern, Mike Richberg, Rob and Tracy Robinson, Tom Shirley (RIP), David Weatherly, Beth Wojiski, Carlston Wood, Colton Woolford, and Craig Woolheater.

And all the witnesses and organizations who graciously shared their experiences.

APPENDIX

Maps

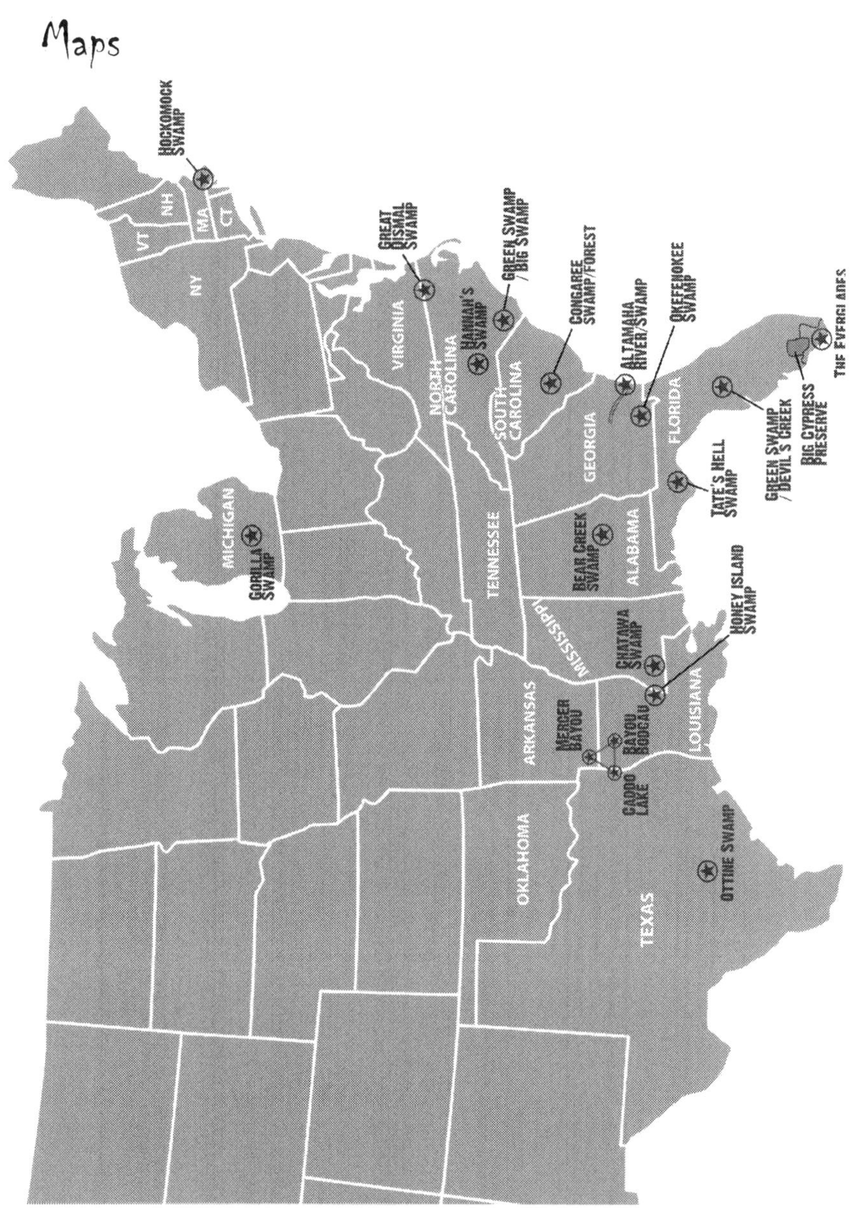

Swamp Locations (full map)

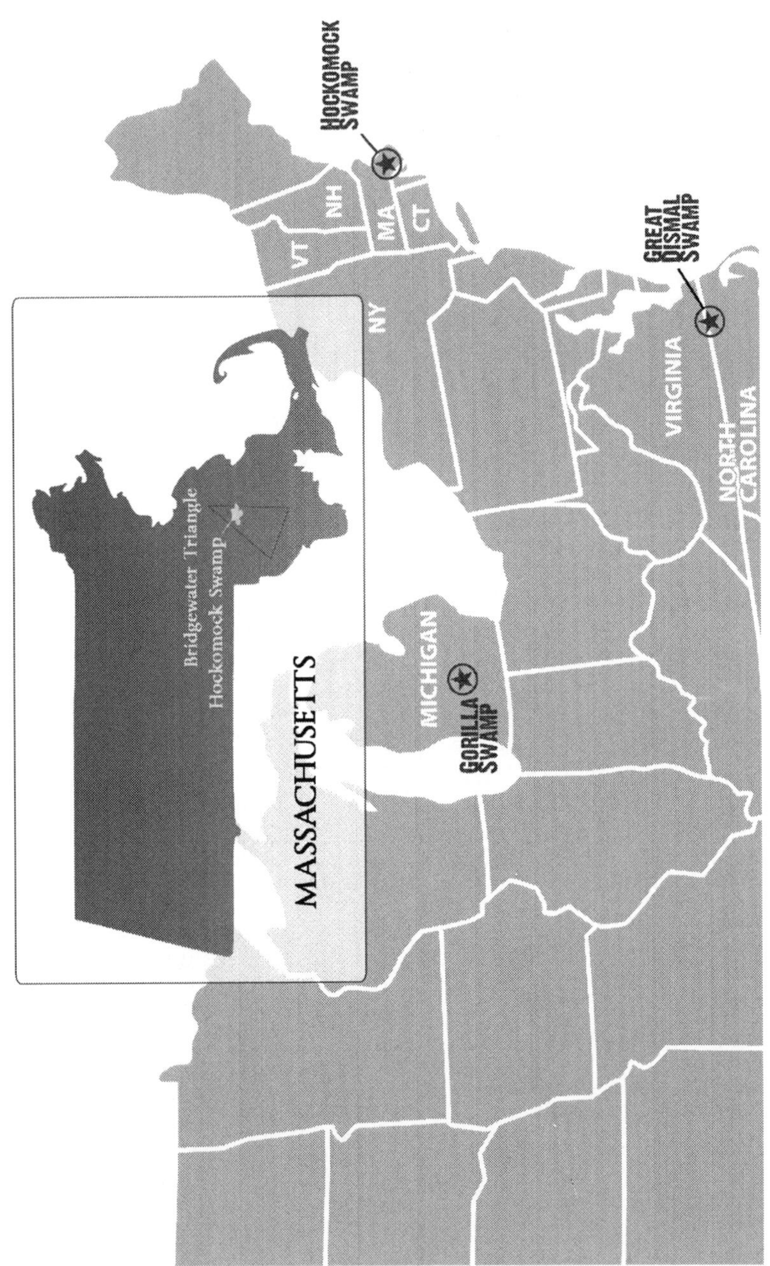

Northern Swamp Detail

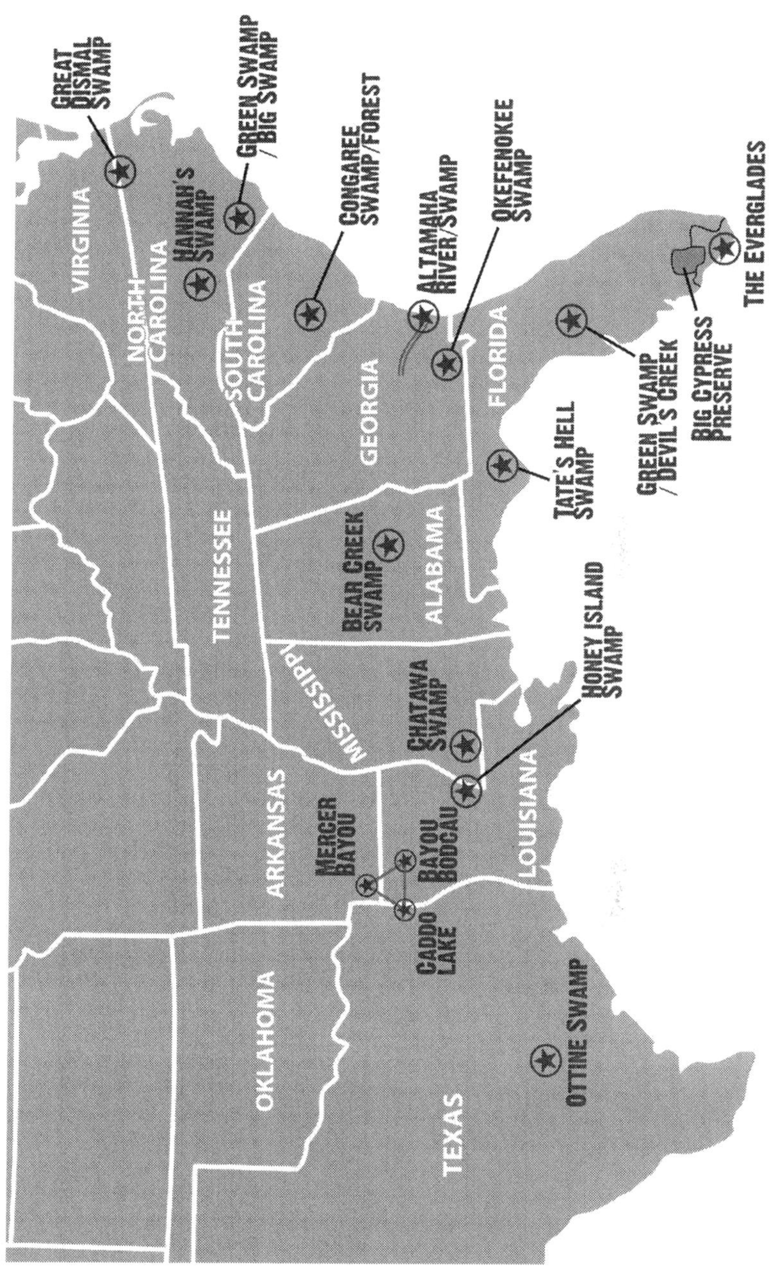

Southern Swamp Detail

Additional Photos

Lyle and Cindy pose with a life-size sculpture of the Altamaha-ha (Altie) by Rick Spears located in the Darien Visitors Center in Darien, Georgia

Lyle at the Ottine Swamp Trail - 2017
(Photo by Sandy Blackburn)

Lyle at Mercer Bayou - 2020
(Photo by Jerry Hestand)

Lyle at age 10 holding a snake at Silver Springs Park in Florida (Cypress Point souvenir photo)

ENDNOTES

1 "Hockomock Swamp ACEC." *Massachusetts Department of Conservation & Recreation*, February 1990, www.mass.gov/service-details/hockomock-swamp-acec

2 Williams, Ted. *Hockomock: Wonder Wetland.* Booklet 1979.

3 Hyman, Rebecca. "Hockomock Swamp can be a devil of a time, especially around Halloween." *Taunton Daily Gazette,* 31 Oct 2011.

4 Coleman, Loren. *Mysterious America: The Ultimate Guide to the Nation's Weirdest Wonders, Strangest Spots, and Creepiest Creatures.* San Antonio. Paraview Pocket Books, 2001, 2007. p. 35.

5 Pittman, Christopher W. "The Bridgewater Triangle: Massachusetts' paranormal 'hot spot.'" www.cellarwalls.com/ufo/btriangle.htm

6 Muscato, Ross A. "Tales from the swamp: From ape-like creatures to glowing lights, Hockomock has kept its secrets for centuries." *The Boston Globe,* 30 Oct 2005.

7 Grace, Tim. "The Bridgewater Triangle." *The Sunday Enterprise,* 30 Oct 2005.

8 Coleman, Loren. *Mysterious America: The Ultimate Guide to the Nation's Weirdest Wonders, Strangest Spots, and Creepiest Creatures.* San Antonio. Paraview Pocket Books, 2001, 2007. p. 39.

9 "America's deadly triangle of terror." *National Examiner,* 16 May 1989.

10 Coleman, Loren. *Mysterious America: The Ultimate Guide to the Nation's Weirdest Wonders, Strangest Spots, and Creepiest Creatures.* San Antonio. Paraview Pocket Books, 2001, 2007. p. 37.

11 *The Bridgewater Triangle.* Co-Directors: Aaron Cadieux and Manny Famolare. Bristol County Media, 2013. DVD.

12 Pittman, Christopher W. "The Bridgewater Triangle: Massachusetts' paranormal 'hot spot.'" www.cellarwalls.com/ufo/btriangle.htm

13 DeAndrade, Joseph M. "My First Sasquatch Sighting in the Bridgewater Triangle." *Paranormal Investigation Organization Newsletter.* (Date unknown.)

14 DeAndrade, Joseph M. "My First Sasquatch Sighting in the Bridgewater Triangle." *Paranormal Investigation Organization Newsletter.* (Date unknown.)

15 *Sasquatch: Out Of The Shadows.* "Bigfoot in the Bridgewater Triangle" (EP 7) https://youtu.be/1PJ6ujBBsz4

16 DeAndrade, Joseph M. "Bridgewater resident investigates unusual happenings." *Capeway News,* 05 Apr 1988.

17 Ibid.

18 Ibid.

19 Hayward, Ed. "The Bigfoot of Bridgewater; Is it a man-beast or Hockomock crock?" *Boston Herald,* 06 Apr 1998.

20 Grace, Tim. "The Bridgewater Triangle." *The Sunday Enterprise,* 30 Oct 2005.

21 "Huge Bird sightings in and a little outside of the B.T." Document on file at the Bridgewater Public Library, Bridgewater, MA.

22 Porrazzo, Jean. "Swamp monsters: Strange sightings are routine in the Bridgewater Triangle." *The Enterprise* 25, Oct 2006.

23 Jim R. "To Joseph DeAndrade." Apr 1988. Letter on file at the Bridgewater Public Library, Bridgewater, MA.

24 "Huge Bird sightings in and a little outside of the B.T." Document on file at the Bridgewater Public Library, Bridgewater, MA.

25 *The Bridgewater Triangle.* Co-Directors: Aaron Cadieux and Manny Famolare. Bristol County Media, 2013. DVD.

26 Russo, Bill. *The Creature From the Bridgewater Triangle and Other Odd Tales From New England.* Self-Published. 2014.

27 "Legendary Native American Figures: Pukwudgie (Puckwudgie)." *Native Languages of the Americas,* www.native-languages.org/pukwudgie.htm

28 Bartel, Bill. "What's in a name? Great Dismal Swamp." *The Virginian-Pilot,* 26 Jul 2010.

29 Traylor, Waverly. *The Great Dismal Swamp in Myth and Legend.* Pennsylvania: RoseDog Books, 2010. p. 76.

30 "Lake of the Dismal Swamp." *Sausalito News,* Vol. 23, No. 3, 19 Jan 1907.

31 "Thomas Moore and Great Dismal Swamp." *All Things Wildly Considered,* June 16, 2013, http://allthingswildlyconsidered.blogspot.com/2013/06/a-ballad-lake-of-dismal-swamp.html

32 Harki, Gary A. "Spooky tales from the Great Dismal Swamp." *The Virginian-Pilot,* 31 Oct 2014.

33 "The Dismal Swamp 'Monster.'" *Richmond Dispatch,* 18 Feb 1902.

34 "Swamp Monster is Killed." *Pittsburg Daily Post,* 13 Apr 1902.

35 "Camden County VA Encounter." *Dogman Encounters,* https://dogmanencounters.com/camden-county-va-encounter

36 "Deer hunter witnesses a large, gorilla like animal." *Bigfoot Field Researchers Organization,* www.bfro.net/GDB/show_report.asp?id=3335

37 Traylor, Waverley. *The Great Dismal Swamp in Myth and Legend.* Pittsburgh: RoseDog Books, 2010. p. 31-32.

38 Ibid, 44-45.

39 "The Mysteries of the Great Dismal Swamp." *North Carolina Ghosts,* https://northcarolinaghosts.com/coast/mysteries-dismal-swamp

40 Grant, Richard. "Deep in the Swamps, Archaeologists Are Finding How Fugitive Slaves Kept Their Freedom." *Smithsonian Magazine,* September 2016, www.smithsonianmag.com/history/deep-swamps-archaeologists-fugitive-slaves-kept-freedom-180960122

41 Traylor, Waverley. *The Great Dismal Swamp in Myth and Legend.* Pittsburgh: RoseDog Books, 2010. p. 29-30.

42 Heimbuch, Jaymi. "See that strange glow in the woods at night? It's foxfire, and it's beautiful." *Mother Nature Network,* July 10, 2017, www.mnn.com/earth-matters/wilderness-resources/stories/foxfire-strange-glow-woods-night

43 Traylor, Waverley. *The Great Dismal Swamp in Myth and Legend.* Pittsburgh: RoseDog Books, 2010. p. 47-48.

44 Ibid, 240-241

45 Ibid, 244-245.

46 Staff writer. "VA. Man Guilty of Murdering His Daughter." *The Washington Post,* 26 Nov 1988.

47 Deluca, Gabriella. "Justin Cornell sentenced 40 years for murder of Brianna Armstrong." *WTKR News 3*, November 16, 2016, https://wtkr.com/2016/11/16/justin-cornell-to-be-sentenced-for-murder-of-brianna-armstrong

48 "Honey Island Swamp." *Wikipedia*, https://en.wikipedia.org/wiki/Honey_Island_Swamp

49 Newsom, Michael. "Sasquatch, rare woodpecker among strange Stennis tales." *Sun Herald*, 26 Oct 2011.

50 Holyfield, Dana. *Honey Island Swamp Monster Documentations: Harlan Ford's Story & More Recent Encounters*. Slidell: Honey Island Swamp Books, 2012.

51 "The Swamp Monster." *In Search Of...*, Alan Landsburg Productions, 1978.

52 "New Species of Monster Seen in South La." *Town Talk*, 24 Oct 1973.

53 "Family witness a large, hair covered creature eating food from their garden." *Bigfoot Field Researchers Organization* (www.bfro.net/GDB/show_report.asp?id=1341) and *John Green Database* (www.sasquatchdatabase.com)

54 "Hunters witness a large, dark, manlike creature pull a stump from the ground." *Bigfoot Field Researchers Organization*, www.bfro.net/GDB/show_report.asp?id=1498

55 Holyfield, Dana. *Honey Island Swamp Monster Documentations: Harlan Ford's Story & More Recent Encounters*. Slidell: Honey Island Swamp Books, 2012.

56 Holyfield, Dana. *Honey Island Swamp Monster Documentations: Harlan Ford's Story & More Recent Encounters*. Slidell: Honey Island Swamp Books, 2012.

57 "Okefenokee Swamp." *Wikipedia*, https://en.wikipedia.org/wiki/Okefenokee_Swamp

58 Andrews, Evan. "The Mysterious Disappearance of Flight 19." *History Channel* website, December 4, 2015, www.history.com/news/the-mysterious-disappearance-of-flight-19

59 Quasar, Gian J. "Me, Flight 19 and the Okefenokee Swamp." *Questersite*, March 31, 2016, https://questersite.wordpress.com/2016/03/31/me-flight-19-and-the-okefenokee-swamp

60 "Two More Gone In Okefenokee: Search Is Abandoned For Servicemen Lost In Georgia Swamp." *News Journal,* 18 Oct 1942.

61 Floyd, E. Randall. "Okefenokee legend a 'beautiful' one." *Anniston Star,* 05 Aug 1990.

62 Ibid.

63 Nelson, Megan Kate. *Trembling Earth: A Cultural History of the Okefenokee Swamp.* Athens. University of Georgia Press, 2005. p. 45.

64 "A Gigantic Story." *Milledgeville (Georgia) Statesman,* June 1929.

65 Miles, Jim. *Weird Georgia: Your Travel Guide to Georgia's Local Legends and Best Kept Secrets.* New York: Sterling Publishing, 2006. p. 23.

66 "Lure and Legends." *Okefenokee* website, www.okefenokee.com/okefenokee_lure-legends

67 Incident 993023. *John Green Database,* www.sasquatchdatabase.com

68 "Lure and Legends." *Okefenokee* website, www.okefenokee.com/okefenokee_lure-legends

69 "Late night sighting by a stranded boater on the St. Marys River." *Bigfoot Field Researchers Organization,* www.bfro.net/GDB/show_report.asp?id=39080

70 "Lure and Legends." *Okefenokee* website, www.okefenokee.com/okefenokee_lure-legends

71 "Late-night sighting by motorist couple between Homerville and Edith." *Bigfoot Field Researchers Organization,* www.bfro.net/GDB/show_report.asp?id=26822

72 "Lure and Legends." *Okefenokee* website, www.okefenokee.com/okefenokee_lure-legends

73 "Was the Okefenokee Swamp once a Native American Venice?" *Okefenokee* website, www.okefenokee.com/nature-history

74 "Lure and Legends." *Okefenokee* website, www.okefenokee.com/okefenokee_lure-legends

75 "Types of Wetlands." United States Environmental Protection Agency publication: EPA 843-F-01-002b, September 2001.

76 Rutledge, Kim, et al. "Swamp." Resource Library. *National Geographic,* www.nationalgeographic.org/encyclopedia/swamp

77 Bond, Courtney. "Creatures Abound at Palmetto State Park—Just Beware the Ottine Swamp Thing." *Texas Monthly* magazine, April 2019.

78 Syers, Ed. *Ghost Stories of Texas*. Texian Press, 1981. pp. 22-25.

79 Frangiamore, Christa S. and Gibbons, Whit. "Altamaha River" *New Georgia Encyclopedia*, www.georgiaencyclopedia.org/articles/geography-environment/altamaha-river

80 Tames, Stephanie. "The Allure of the Altamaha." *Nature Conservancy Magazine*, Autumn 2012.

81 Frangiamore, Christa S. and Gibbons, Whit. "Altamaha River" *New Georgia Encyclopedia*, www.georgiaencyclopedia.org/articles/geography-environment/altamaha-river

82 "Savannah: Thursday Morning April 22." *Savannah Georgian*, 23 Apr 1830.

83 "News." *Charleston Mercury*, 29 Mar 1830.

84 Davis, Ann R. "Sightings of the 'Altamaha-Ha' or river creature of Darien, GA." *Rhett Davis* website, 1996, http://rhettdavisboy.angelfire.com/sighting.htm

85 Ibid.

86 Ibid.

87 Ibid.

88 Ibid.

89 Ibid.

90 Ibid.

91 "Legendary Native American Figures: Tie-Snake." *Native Languages*, http://www.native-languages.org/morelegends/tie-snake.htm

92 Michaels, Denver. "The Altamaha-ha." *Denver Michaels* website, December 27, 2017, www.denvermichaels.net/the-altamaha-ha

93 Davis, Ann R. "Sightings of the 'Altamaha-Ha' or river creature of Darien, GA." *Rhett Davis* website, 1996, http://rhettdavisboy.angelfire.com/sighting.htm

94 "After two years of lying low, Altamaha-ha was sighted." *Darien News*, 03 Feb 1983.

95 Davis, Ann R. "Sightings of the 'Altamaha-Ha' or river creature of Darien, GA." *Rhett Davis* website, 1996, http://rhettdavisboy.angelfire.com/sighting.htm

96 Russell, Kathleen. "Eel-like sea creature makes appearance again." *Darien News,* 26 May 1988.

97 Cox, Dale. "Altamaha-ha - Sea Monster of the Georgia Coast." *Explore Southern History,* April 22, 2017, www.exploresouthernhistory.com/altamahaha.html

98 Leake, Danae. "Carcass of strange sea creature washes up on Georgia beach." *WSB-TV 2 Atlanta,* 19 Mar 2018.

99 "Multiple witness sighting near Beards Creek Church, outside Glennville." *Bigfoot Field Researchers Organization,* www.bfro.net/GDB/show_report.asp?id=2279

100 "Hunter has a late-afternoon encounter near the Altamaha River." *Bigfoot Field Researchers Organization,* www.bfro.net/GDB/show_report.asp?id=27072

101 Rutledge, Kim, et al. "Swamp." *National Geographic,* www.nationalgeographic.org/encyclopedia/swamp

102 "Plants." Everglades National Park, Florida. *National Park Service,* www.nps.gov/ever/learn/nature/plants.htm

103 Miaschi, John. "The Animals of the Florida Everglades." *WorldAtlas,* August 29, 2017, www.worldatlas.com/articles/what-animals-live-in-the-everglades.html

104 Kaye, Ken. "Flight 19: Has mystery of Lost Patrol been solved?" *Sun Sentinel,* 07 Apr 2014.

105 Staff writer. "Plane Found In Everglades Fails To Shed Light On 'Lost Patrol.'" *Chicago Tribune,* 02 Jul 1989.

106 Kaye, Ken. "Solving mystery of 'Lost City' in Everglades." *Sun Sentinel,* 18 May 2014.

107 O'Connor, John. "The Legend of Chokoloskee." *Oxford American* (magazine), Issue No. 90, Nov 2015.

108 Swancer, Brent. "The Myriad Mysteries of the Florida Everglades." *Mysterious Universe,* January 12, 2016, https://mysteriousuniverse.org/2016/01/the-myriad-mysteries-of-the-florida-everglades

109 "No Trace Of Man Missing 30 Days In Everglades Park." *CBS4 Miami*, April 5, 2011, https://miami.cbslocal.com/2011/04/05/no-trace-of-man-missing-30-days-in-everglades-park

110 "Park Service Ends Search For Missing Everglades Visitor." *CBS4 Miami*, September 10, 2011, https://miami.cbslocal.com/2011/09/10/park-service-ends-search-for-missing-everglades-visitor

111 Swancer, Brent. "Come Fly the Haunted Skies!" *Mysterious Universe*, February 13, 2015, https://mysteriousuniverse.org/2015/02/come-fly-the-haunted-skies

112 Ibid.

113 Swancer, Brent. "The Myriad Mysteries of the Florida Everglades." *Mysterious Universe*, January 12, 2016, https://mysteriousuniverse.org/2016/01/the-myriad-mysteries-of-the-florida-everglades

114 Jonesblue. "The Everglades Ghost Boy." *Your Ghost Stories*, www.yourghoststories.com/real-ghost-story.php?story=4994

115 Green, John. *Sasquatch: The Apes Among Us*. Washington/Vancouver: Hancock House, 1978. pp. 271-272.

116 Cox, Dale. "The Wild Man of Ocheesee Pond – Jackson, County, Florida." *Explore Southern History*, March 10, 2014, www.exploresouthernhistory.com/ocheeseewildman.html

117 C.L. Murphy. *Sasquatch/Bigfoot Chronicle*. Unpublished, 2013. Obtained from *Sasquatch Canada* website (http://www.sasquatchcanada.com). p 7.

118 Bothwell, Dick. "'Skunk Ape' in the Everglades – A Hairy Giant That Smells Bad." *National Observer*, 16 Aug 1971.

119 "Skunk Ape Spotted." *Sarasota Journal*, 09 Aug 1971.

120 Bothwell, Dick. "'Skunk Ape' in the Everglades – A Hairy Giant That Smells Bad." *National Observer*, 16 Aug 1971.

121 Coleman, Loren. "Mysterious World: The Myakka Skunk Ape Photographs." *FATE Magazine*, May 2001: 8-11.

122 "Big-Footed Monsters Invade Earth." *National News Explorer*, 13 August 1972.

123 Kelly, Jim. "Creature Feature." *Miami News*, 19 Feb 1998.

124 Glass, Ian and Jon Hall. "'Skunk Ape' on Prowl? Glades Creature Sought." *Miami News*, 09 Jan 1974.

125 Ibid.

126 Kelly, Jim. "Creature Feature." *Miami News,* 19 Feb 1998.

127 Report #72168-1. Dade County Public Safety Department, March 24, 1975.

128 "Early morning encounter during a rest stop near Florida City." *Bigfoot Field Researchers Organization,* www.bfro.net/GDB/show_report.asp?id=36218

129 Kelly, Jim. "Creature Feature." *Miami News,* 19 Feb 1998.

130 "Series of reports (6) concerning the Skunk Ape." *Bigfoot Field Researchers Organization,* www.bfro.net/gdb/show_report.asp?id=721

131 Tiansay, Eric. "Panther Tracker Claims Bigfoot Sighting." *Naples Daily News* (Florida), 20 Nov 1998.

132 "Driver spots a tall biped crossing the road just west of Miami." *Bigfoot Field Researchers Organization,* www.bfro.net/GDB/show_report.asp?id=38893

133 "Daylight sighting of a man-like ape while target shooting in the Big Cypress National Preserve." *Bigfoot Field Researchers Organization,* www.bfro.net/GDB/show_report.asp?id=37203

134 "Hunters in the Big Cypress National Preserve observe large biped traversing their recent path." *Bigfoot Field Researchers Organization,* www.bfro.net/GDB/show_report.asp?id=45566

135 "The paid hunters dealing with Florida's python problem." *CBS News,* May 17, 2017, www.cbsnews.com/news/python-problem-hunters-everglades

136 Marshall, John. "The Myth of Florida's Monster Snake." *Medium News,* September 9, 2017, https://medium.com/@marshall.katheder/the-myth-of-floridas-monster-snake-699a089d5efe

137 "The paid hunters dealing with Florida's python problem." *CBS News,* May 17, 2017, www.cbsnews.com/news/python-problem-hunters-everglades/

138 Bancroft, Jacoby. "Creepy Stories And Legends About The Florida Everglades." *Graveyard Shift,* www.ranker.com/list/creepy-everglades-stories/jacobybancroft

139 Godfrey, Linda S. *American Monsters: A History of Monster Lore, Legends, and Sightings in America*. New York: Tarcher / Penguin Books, 2014. pp. 147-159.

140 Duguid, Julian. *Green Hell: A Chronicle of Travel in the Forests of Eastern Bolivia*. New York: Century Co, 1931.

141 "Tate's Hell State Forest." Florida Department of Agriculture and Consumer Services, Florida Forest Service Fact Sheet DACS-P-00175 Rev. 1, 2014.

142 Sanders, Debra S. "The Legend of Tate's Hell." *Debra Sanders* website, November 3, 2016, https://debsanders.com/2016/11/03/the-legend-of-tates-hell

143 Laufenberg, Kathleen. "Florida's Monster." *Tallahassee Democrat,* 14 Aug 2005.

144 Green, John. *Sasquatch: The Apes Among Us*. Washington/Vancouver: Hancock House, 1978. p. 200.

145 "'Beast' Lurks In State Area." *The Michigan Daily*, 14 Jul 1950.

146 "Motorist has nighttime sighting of animal near Marshall." *Bigfoot Field Researchers Organization,* www.bfro.net/GDB/show_report.asp?id=10151

147 Edwards, Mika and Kimberly Solet. "Tales from the Swamp." *The Courier* (Terrebonne Parish, Louisiana), 30 Oct 2005.

148 "Devils Swamp Lake: A Review Of Fish Data." U.S. Department Of Health And Human Services, Public Health Service Agency for Toxic Substances and Disease Registry Division *cdc.gov* website, August 29, 2006, https://www.atsdr.cdc.gov/HAC/pha/DevilsSwampLake/DevilsSwampLakeHC082906.pdf

149 Wooten, Patty. "Seven Devils: The wildlife paradise with the ominous name." *SEARK Today*, January 29, 2013, https://searktoday.com/seven-devils-wildlife-paradise-with-the-foreboding-name

150 Spear, Kevin. "Haunting Legend of Green Swamp." *The Orlando Sentinel,* 31 Oct 1991.

151 Charlton, Linda. "Homestead in Green Swamp Was Site of Slayings in 1918." *The Reporter,* 25 Oct 2009.

152 "Twilight sighting on the west side of Lakeland." *Bigfoot Field Researchers Organization,* www.bfro.net/GDB/show_report.asp?id=11812

153 White, Gary. "Woman's Sighting of Ape-Like Green Swamp Creature Among the Theories Studied by Cryptozoologists." *The Ledger,* 13 Nov 2004.

154 "Hunter watches creature picking persimmons in the Green Swamp." *Bigfoot Field Researchers Organization,* www.bfro.net/GDB/show_report.asp?id=25129

155 Robinson, Robert C. *Legend Tripping: The Ultimate Family Experience.* Genie Publishing, 2017.

156 "Possible nighttime encounter experienced by campers in the West Tract of the Green Swamp Preserve." *Bigfoot Field Researchers Organization,* www.bfro.net/GDB/show_report.asp?id=32308

157 White, Gary. "Wife Wonders What Became of Husband in the Green Swamp." *The Ledger,* 27 Feb 2006.

158 Downing, Sarah. "Green Swamp Preserve Offers Unique Nature Opportunity. *Life In Brunswick County,* July 17, 2018, https://lifeinbrunswick-county.com/green-swamp-preserve-offers-unique-nature-opportunity

159 "Mystery Beast Slays Dogs of Bladenboro." *Wilmington News,* 03 Jan 1954.

160 "Woman Eludes Bleeder Beast In Attack At Bladenboro Home." *Asheville Citizen Times,* 06 Jan 1954.

161 Ibid.

162 "Death Traps Are Laid For 'Vampire Beast.'" *Asheville Citizen Times,* 07 Jan 1954.

163 "Reports Of Strange Beasts In N.C. Common; Beasts Aren't." *Asheville Citizen Times,* 17 Jan 1954.

164 "Woman Eludes Bleeder Beast In Attack At Bladenboro Home." *Asheville Citizen Times,* 06 Jan 1954.

165 "Beast Of Bladenboro Seen Again." *The Daily Tar Heel,* 13 Jan 1954.

166 "Bobcat Shot; May Have Been Vampire Beast." *Asheville Citizen Times,* 14 Jan 1954.

167 "Big Dog Is Suspected As Bladen 'Beast'" *Asheville Citizen Times,* 13 Jan 1954.

168 "Two More Suspects Enter Bladen 'Vampire' Gallery. *The Robesonian,* 14 Jan 1954.

169 "Welcome to Bayou Bodcau Dam & Reservoir." *US Army Corps of Engineers Vicksburg District,* www.mvk.usace.army.mil/Missions/Recreation/Bayou-Bodcau

170 Farmer, Patsi. "The Mysterious 'Eel.'" *The Shreveport Times,* 17 Aug 1958.

171 "Daylight sighting by squirrel hunter outside Sarepta." *Bigfoot Field Researchers Organization,* www.bfro.net/GDB/show_report.asp?id=23227

172 "The Caddo Lake History Page." *Caddo Lake,* www.caddolake.com/history.htm

173 "Marion County 'Monster' Recalls 1927 Experience." *The Longview News Journal,* 09 Sept 1965.

174 Power, Irvin. "Boy Says For Real Sighting of Monster Renews Marion Legend." *Marshall News Messenger,* 01 Sept. 1965.

175 "Town Fed Up With Monster Hunters." *United Press International,* 20 Sept 1965.

176 "Deer hunter encounters bigfoot at Caddo Lake near Karnack." *Bigfoot Field Researchers Organization,* www.bfro.net/GDB/show_report.asp?id=8067

177 Ingham, Donna. *Mysteries and Legends of Texas: True Stories of the Unsolved and Unexplained.* Morris Book Publishing, LLC, 2010.

178 Crabtree, J.E. Smokey. *Smokey and the Fouke Monster.* Fouke: Days Creek Production Corporation, 1974.

179 "Miller Co. AR sighting report." *Texas Bigfoot Center* website archives, (no longer online).

180 "Coon hunter and dogs experience close encounter in Sulphur River bottoms between Doddridge and Fouke." *North American Wood Ape Conservancy*, February 11, 2004, http://woodape.org/reports/report/detail/349

181 Ibid.

182 Rabil, Carter. "An 1865 Johnston County Ghost Story." *The Johnston County Report*, October 31, 2017, https://jocoreport.com/an-1865-johnston-county-ghost-story

183 Herndon, Ernest. "Chatawa's 'Bigfoot' – Man, monster, or joke?" *Enterprise-Journal,* 07 Dec 1980.

184 Herndon, Ernest. "Monkey sighting joins list of Chatawa stories. *Enterprise-Journal,* 22 Feb 1998.

185 "7 most terrifying places in Alabama, as seen on TV." *Alabama* website, posted Oct 10, 2013; updated Jan 14, 2019, www.al.com/living/2013/10/7_most_terrifying_places_in_al.html

186 Crider, Beverly. *Legends and Lore of Birmingham & Central Alabama.* The History Press, March 18, 2014

187 Davis, Judd. "Paranormal investigator makes stop at haunted Prattville spot." October 27, 2017, www.wsfa.com/story/36700935/paranormal-investigator-makes-stop-at-haunted-prattville-spot

188 "Bear Creek Swamp." *ignitetheunderground* blog, October 24, 2011, https://ignitetheunderground.wordpress.com/2011/10/24/bear-creek-swamp

189 Sarafin, Faith. *Haunted Montgomery, Alabama.* The History Press, August 20, 2013.

190 Roney, Marty. "Creepy doll graveyard found in Alabama swamp." *USA Today* via *Montgomery (Ala.) Advertiser* 26 Nov 2014

191 "See the Largest Expanse of Old-Growth Hardwoods in the U.S." *National Geographic*, November 5, 2009, www.nationalgeographic.com/travel/national-parks/congaree-national-park

192 Bronaugh, Whit "Congaree: Where The Trees Are Still Tall." *American Forests* magazine, Summer 2009.

193 "Congaree Swamps: The Swamp Lady – Columbia, SC." *American Ghost Stories*, date unknown, https://americanghoststories.com/southern-ghost-stories/the-swamp-lady-columbia-sc

194 Cantelmi, Dayna. "Get Your Ghost On at 7 of Columbia SC's Spookiest Haunts." *Experience Columbia SC*, October 17, 2017, www.experiencecolumbiasc.com/blog/post/get-your-ghost-on-at-8-of-columbia-scs-spookiest-haunts

195 C.L. Murphy. *Sasquatch/Bigfoot Chronicle.* Unpublished, 2013. Obtained from *Sasquatch Canada* website (http://www.sasquatchcanada.com). pp 6-7.

196 "Shambling Beast Terrorizes Town: Hairy Animal Reported In South Carolina Village." *The Daily Gleaner,* 09 Feb 1938.

197 "Solider describes late night encounter on Fort Jackson." *Bigfoot Field Researchers Organization*, www.bfro.net/GDB/show_report.asp?id=5381

INDEX

H

L

M

N

O

P

ABOUT THE AUTHOR

Lyle Blackburn is a native Texan known for his work in writing, music, and film. His investigative books reflect his life-long fascination with cryptid creatures and spooky legends. Lyle has been heard on numerous radio programs, including *Coast To Coast AM*, and has been featured on television shows such as *Monsters and Mysteries in America*, *Finding Bigfoot*, and *Strange Evidence*. Lyle is also the frontman for the rock band Ghoultown, and narrator/host of Small Town Monsters documentary films, including *Boggy Creek Monster*, *The Mothman of Point Pleasant*, *Bray Road Beast*, *Terror in the Skies*, and more.

When Lyle isn't writing books, chasing cryptids, or performing with his band, he can be found speaking at various cryptozoology conferences and horror conventions around the United States. Just look for the trademark black cowboy hat.

For more information, visit www.lyleblackburn.com

MORE BOOKS BY THE AUTHOR

The Beast of Boggy Creek:
The True Story of the Fouke Monster

Beyond Boggy Creek:
In Search of the Southern Sasquatch

Lizard Man:
The True Story of the Bishopville Monster

Momo:
The Strange Case of the Missouri Monster

Monstro Bizarro:
An Essential Manual of Mysterious Monsters

legend
SCAPE

Made in the USA
Monee, IL
03 June 2021